GRACE THEOLOGY

FOR MISSIONAL CHURCH

ABI OLOWE

PUBLISHED BY
OMEGA PUBLISHERS
HOUSTON, TEXAS, U.S.A.

All Biblical quotations are from King James Version (www.scripturegroup.net).
All Bible commentaries are from Life Application Study Bible, KJV, Tyndale House Publishers, Inc.

First Printed: 2009

ISBN 978-0-9795299-5-5

Cover Design: B-Links, Inc (www.b-links.com)

Printed in United States of America

For further enquiries, please contact
Omega Publishers USA
Tel.: 281-744-5033

TO God our father, Jesus Christ His son and our savior, and to the Holy Spirit our guidance and counselor

PREFACE

DURING my first trip to the Embassy of God Church in Ukraine in August 2008, a prophecy I received earlier that I was going to receive revelations from God, began to materialize. Since then, I have been overwhelmed with revelations and Spiritual inspiration enough to write several books. My first book since I started this project, "*Missional Reformation*", is in two volumes and I had to jump over to write this book in parallel before I forgot some important revelations. At a point, I locked myself in my office for several days without talking to anyone. God wants to reform His Church and I am grateful that He counts me worthy to be used. I am a Materials Science Engineer by learning and a University Professor and Computer Programmer by career. I had to give up a lot of comforts in order to fully concentrate on this project. Theology has never been my profession, but God has called me into it as if it is. I am sure, reading this book will convince you too. I have never been to a Bible College and I started seriously to study the Bible in 2003 at the beginning of my first book, "*Great Revivals*", published in 2007.

During my research and writing of this book, I realized that the *doctrine of grace* is the basic doctrine in Christianity. There seems to be an impasse that has been hanging around theological debate for over 400 years, to the extent that it has caused non believing philosophers in the society to infiltrate into spiritual matters. The Church should have a common and acceptable doctrine of grace to be able to speak with one voice. It is unfortunate that during the development of the doctrine of grace in the history of the Church, schisms occurred. There are several errors in the existing doctrines, and I will address some of them in this book.

I will recommend that whoever is reading this *Grace Theology* book buys a copy of "*Missional Reformation*". As a package, they complement each other. You may want to use these books in academic settings, Bible studies, or as conference materials.

> For though I preach the Gospel, I have nothing to glory of: for necessity is laid upon me; yea, woe is unto me, if I preach not the Gospel!" (1 Cor. 9:16)

The faith of this generation is of concern to me.

Abi Olowe, Ph.D.
Houston, Texas

ACKNOWLEDGEMENTS

I THANK our Lord Jesus Christ, the author of our faith and the good shepherd who orders my steps and who initiated me into this project.

My gratitude goes to Pastor Sunday Adelaja who God has used as the vehicle to this project. I thank my dear brother, Pastor Joseph Olowe (MD), and Ladi and Keni Omole for their moral support.

I must also thank the editorial staff, especially LaTonya Pegues and my reviewers for their special interest in this project.

CONTENTS

INTRODUCTION

I AM an ardent student of biblical numbers and their significances. I use the number 7 quite often towards perfection and the number 40 for long suffering. The number 2 is new to me and I noticed it during this project. God creates things in pairs to help, or to assist, or to complement each other. God created Eve for this purpose. Moses received the Ten Commandments of God in two slabs of stone and God revealed in *Missional Reformation* (Olowe 2009) that the two slabs represent the Gospel of His Kingdom in two parts: Salvation and Good works; they complement each other through His grace which also forms a pair: Universal Grace and Special Grace. The pair of grace complements each other. One of the objectives of this book is to elaborate on the grace of God in two parts.

The Old Testament ends with Malachi and the New Testaments starts with Matthew; the gap between the two Testaments is roughly over 400 years. So, for over 400 years, there was no major Spiritual activity in Israel. God was silent, watching His people. The Calvinist doctrine of grace, developed during the second stage of the Protestant Reformation, is now roughly over 400 years old. God has not intervened until now; God is now talking. It is time for a change. The doctrine of grace developed in this book is no doubt applicable to the postmodern movements which the Calvinist doctrine denies. Calvinism is telling us that God has predestinated some people for Heaven and some for hell which means that evangelizing is not necessary; otherwise how would you tell someone that "although God may not have elected you for Heaven, but you should accept Jesus all the same"? Although there have been variants of the doctrine, it is still based on a shaky foundation.

In the writing of this book, I prayed on every topic and sought the guidance of the Holy Spirit. Whatever wisdom I might have acquired or used belongs to God as we shall see that He is the owner of everything. Also, I need to reiterate that I am an engineer-scientist and not a philosopher. I have consulted only the Bible, Christian books, Christian articles, and sometimes the dictionary.

In as much as I disagree with the doctrine of double predestination by the Calvinists, there are areas of common agreement such as in the doctrine of depravity of man and the sovereignty of God. However, I believe there are some little exaggerations in both doctrines. Many have written on the relationship between the Church and the society, wondering and asking why the Church is not imparting the society. Well, one of the reasons is the result of the controversial Calvinists' doctrine of grace; it created holier-than-thou Christians who think they are "elected" to Heaven and who do not want to associate with the "sinful" society. This should remind us of the parable of the Good Samaritan. One of the current powerful revelations from God was His response to Landa Cope's inquiry. She explains how God revealed to her: "*the devastation you see [in Africa] is the fruit of preaching salvation alone without the rest of the biblical message*. This quotation stands out in "*Missional Reformation*" (Olowe 2009).

Reformation is not complete without a *doctrine of grace*. This book, without planning for it, has become the "Volume 3" of the *Missional Reformation* series. We are in a new generation; a generation of discipling nations; a generation of implementing good works. This new generation has to be equipped with a sound doctrine of grace. The doctrine in this book (it is open to improvement) is written with the guidance of the Holy Spirit and it has several elements of God's revelations. There are three important revelatory diagrammatic illustrations that have been very helpful in writing *Grace Theology*:

Figure 8.2: The Gospel of the Kingdom (Chapter 8);
Figure 4.5: Triune state of a regenerate man (Chapter 4);
Figure 9.1: Path to Eternal Kingdom (Chapter 9).

This book, *Grace Theology*, examines all the manifestations of the Grace of God. It presents the basic doctrine of grace for a Missional Church. Come along as we explore and learn the revelations of God for this generation.

1. HISTORY OF GRACE DOCTRINE

HISTORICALLY, the doctrine of grace has gone through different cycles starting from the first century before the first Ecumenical Council at Jerusalem in 50 AD. We can say that there have been four major stages in the development of the doctrine of grace; this current one being the fifth. The four previous stages are:

Stage 1: 1st century Apostles;
Stage 2: 5th century Augustine-Pelagius;
Stage 3: 16th century Protestant Reformers;
Stage 4: 19th century Kuyper's common grace.

We will study the events in these four stages.

FIRST CENTURY DOCTRINES

The first century was dominated by activities of the Apostles. Most of their writings were focused on the doctrine of faith in Christ Jesus. It is quite understandable because Jesus just left them and they had to make Christ acceptable to people. The Apostles laid the foundation of the various doctrines of salvation that are still being debated today. Before Paul was converted, the foundational Apostles had established much of the principal doctrines of faith and grace, and were commonly accepted and applied by all believers.

PAUL AND PETER

There were tensions within the early Christian communities especially between Christians of Jewish background and Christians of Gentile background as can be seen from the epistles to the Romans, Galatians and Ephesians. The first major hurdle in the development of the doctrine of grace was to quell this tension; the major actors were Peter, Paul, and James, the brother of Jesus.

Paul, who was not one of the Foundational Apostles, was very active, being sent to minister to the Gentiles. Paul fiercely debated the Foundational Apostles due to what looked like hypocrisy of the early Jewish Christians trying to separate themselves from the Gentiles, what Jesus would not have done; Jesus ate with sinners.

> But when Peter was come to Antioch, I withstood him to the face, because he was to be blamed. For before that certain came from James, he did eat with the Gentiles: but when they were come, he withdrew and separated himself, fearing them which were of the circumcision
> Gal 2: 11-12

The first major issue was the acceptance of the "uncircumcised" in the fold of believers. It seemed that the Jewish Christians were initially trying to protect the new faith. They believed that a gentile needed to first follow the ceremonial laws (Lev. 1-7) and Jewish traditions before becoming a Christian.

> And certain men which came down from Judaea taught the brethren, and said, Except ye be circumcised after the manner of Moses, ye cannot be saved. When therefore Paul and Barnabas had no small dissension and disputation with them, they determined that Paul and Barnabas, and certain other of them, should go up to Jerusalem unto the apostles and elders about this question.
> Acts 15: 1-2 (see also Acts 15:5)

The issue was resolved at the Ecumenical Council in Jerusalem in about 50 AD (Acts 15). At the Jerusalem Council, the key issue was that salvation is by grace through faith and not by the works of the law. Peter was the one who spoke first to accept the Gentiles without following Jewish laws (Acts 15:9-11). James, who took a lead role in this discussion, did not disagree with Peter or Paul over this crucial matter.

PAUL AND JAMES

The doctrine of grace that has generated debates up till today stems from the writings of Paul and James in about 49 AD. What seems to be the conflict of statements is found in the books of Galatians, James, and Romans, written in that order. Rather than contradicting each other, it seems that James wrote (after the Galatians) to correct some misinterpretations of Paul's teachings by some of the early Christians. According to the Application Bible, both the book of James and Galatians were written approximately in 49 AD before the Jerusalem Council and Romans was written after the Council in about 57 AD.

Today, many people still (mis)interpret both Paul and James as having contradicting statements about faith and works. In actual fact, the contradiction between Paul and James is only apparent; it is not real. The major bone of contention is found in the two verses below:

> Therefore we conclude that a man is justified by faith without the deeds of the law. Rom. 3: 28
>
> Ye see then how that by works a man is justified, and not by faith only. James 2: 24

Both Paul and James are speaking to different audiences; their emphases are also different. Paul stresses that the foundation of our salvation is the death of Jesus, not the laws of Moses. James stresses that Christians must put their faith into action.

Dr. Felix Just and The Middletown Bible Church provide good analyses to dismiss the apparent conflict.

1. Paul and James had different perspectives. Paul is speaking to the unsaved man on how he might get right with God. James is focusing on how a saved person could show that his faith is real.
2. Both agree that no one can be justified by doing the law. The law does not save, because no one is able to perfectly fulfill it (Rom 3:20 and Jas 2:10).
3. Paul teaches that “works of law” are unnecessary but James teaches that “good works” are essential. Paul was speaking of those works (of ceremonial laws) that an unsaved person tries to do in order to win salvation; the works include all kinds of sacrifices (peace, sin, burnt offerings) and Jewish laws on circumcision; Paul says "works of the Law" (Gal 2:16; 3:2-12; Rom 3:28). James on the other hand refers to those good works that a saved person performs.
4. Paul did not use the word "alone" in Rom 3:28; Martin Luther was the one who added it in his translation. James does not write "by works alone" but stresses "not by faith alone"; he maintains that both have to go together. James does not teach that good works are necessary in order to gain salvation and Paul never teaches that good works are unnecessary after a person is saved. On the contrary, Paul agrees with James that for the person justified by faith, good works are essential (Phil. 2:12-13; Titus 3:5-8; Eph. 2:8-10, Gal 5–6; Rom 12–15). Likewise, James

agrees with Paul that faith is a necessary condition for inheriting the Kingdom (James 2:5, 14-26)

5. James did not contradict Paul at the Jerusalem Council of Acts 15, where he could have seized the opportunity.
6. Interestingly, to argue their points, both James and Paul appealed to the example of Abraham in Gen 15:6, but in a different way. Paul was trying to argue (Rom 4:1-3, 10-12) that Abraham believed God, and it was reckoned to him as righteousness, not after, but before he was circumcised. James 2:21-23 says "*Was not our ancestor Abraham justified by works when he offered his son Isaac on the altar?* (Gen 22:9-18). In other words, Paul argues that Abraham was justified (in Gen 15) before he was circumcised (in Gen 17), while James argues that Abraham's faith in God was completed and evidenced by his willingness to sacrifice his son Isaac (in Gen 22).

The issue of Justification will be discussed in Chapter 9.

HERESIES

Most of the epistles were written to combat false teachings. The Apostles battle false teachings that crept into the early Church especially due to misinterpretations of Paul's teachings. For example, to the Collose church:

> And this I say, lest any man should beguile you with enticing words. Col. 2:4

To the Galatians

> I marvel that ye are so soon removed from him that called you into the grace of Christ unto another Gospel: Which is not another; but there be some that trouble you, and would pervert the Gospel of Christ. Gal. 1: 6 -7

Some false teachers in the church in Corinth questioned Paul's authority and slandered him. These "chiefest apostles" (2 Cor 11:5) preached a Gospel of spiritual self-fulfillment. Paul wrote 2 Corinthians to defend his ministry and to denounce those who were twisting the truth.

> And no marvel; for satan himself is transformed into an angel of light. Therefore it is no great thing if his ministers also be transformed as the ministers of righteousness; whose end shall be according to their works. 2 Cor. 11:14-15

Peter had to be writing to warn Christians in Rome about opportunists using Paul's writings to justify their sins. Peter politely wrote to them that some of Paul's writings are difficult to crack:

> And account that the longsuffering of our Lord is salvation; even as our beloved brother Paul also according to the wisdom given unto him hath written unto you; As also in all his epistles, speaking in them of these things; in which are some things hard to be understood, which they that are unlearned and unstable wrest, as they do also the other scriptures, unto their own destruction. 2Pet 3: 15-16

By the time of Peter's writing, Paul's letters were already widely circulated in Rome. The letter to the Romans was written about 10 years before 2 Peter and about 7 years before First Peter. Here is the Application Bible's comment on the verses:

> The false teachers intentionally misused Paul's writings by twisting them to condone lawlessness. No doubt this made the teachers popular, because people always like to have their favorite sins justified, but the net effect was to totally destroy Paul's message... Peter warns his readers to avoid those wicked teachers by growing in the knowledge of Jesus. The better we know Jesus, the less attractive false teachings will be.

False teachings being generated around Paul's writings are still found in the Church till today.

FIFTH CENTURY DOCTRINES

AUGUSTINE AND PELAGIUS

The teaching of Pelagius, a monk from Wales, was almost unknown to the Church until Augustine brought it up. There was no attention on Pelagius teaching mainly because the focus at that time was on the doctrine of Trinity and deity and humanity of Jesus which took the Church a long stretch. Augustine of Hippo (354-430) was also prominent in the debate on the doctrine of the Trinity, and in most other issues of the period. He is generally recognized as the greatest thinker of Christian antiquity (Britannica), the Father of Western theology, and the father of Roman Catholicism. Augustine criticized Pelagius' teaching.

In 405 AD, reacting to a quotation in Augustine's work "*Confessions*", that God's will was his command, Pelagius argued that God cannot command what a man does not have the ability do; he further stated that man has free will and is able to choose good from evil. He would take responsibilities for his own sins but not those of Adam. Augustine responded with five major points: original sin, total depravity, unconditional election, irresistible grace, and perseverance of the saints. The debate between Pelagius and Augustine is summarized in Table 2.1.

Table 2.1: Pelagius-Augustine Debate

Pelagius	Augustine
Man does not inherit the original sin from Adam and he is not guilty of Adam's sin.	**Original Sin:** Adam's sin is transmitted to his descendants. Each human inherits the guilt of sin from his parents, starting from Adam.
Each person is born as a new, free agent with no sin and the same powers of choice and responsibilities as Adam. Man has free will and is able to choose good from evil.	**Total Depravity:** Man is inherently corrupted by sin in every aspect of his being. Because of this guilt, man lacks free will to choose God, and renders Adam and his descendants not able not to sin. The freedom of the will to act is not in question, and man still makes his choices. However, his choices are all determined now by his corrupt nature, and in himself he has no ability to choose God (Salvation).

Pelagius	Augustine
Man has the ability to be free from sin.	**Unconditional Election:** The free grace of God is apparently necessary since man cannot choose Him. God's grace grants everything, so election cannot be based on foreseen future merits. **Irresistible Grace:** Grace and predestination cannot be separated. Predestination is the preparation, and grace the actual application, of God's unmerited favor. **Perseverance of the Saints:** After death the redeemed saints are finally confirmed in a state which Adam did not enjoy, namely, not able to sin. None of the elect could finally fall away.

AUGUSTINE AND SEMI-PELAGIANISM

John Cassian developed a middle view which later came to be called Semi-Pelagianism. He agreed that men have a moral nature so far tainted by depravity that this indispensable process cannot in any instance be carried through without a supernatural gracious work of God's Spirit upon them. But he insisted that a man has the freedom to resist the grace of God. He found a middle ground on free will, explaining that man's will was able to choose God, though perhaps only able to do that; upon choosing God, God gives cooperating grace to enable a person to complete the process of becoming a Christian. Therefore faith is not truly a gift of God. Moreover, God's election is based upon a foreknowledge of future actions on the part of each human being, so He chooses whom he foreknows will believe (William Cunningham).

Augustine responded and reaffirmed that faith and perseverance are gifts of God. Even the very beginning of faith, the first tiny steps of faith, even the thinking and willing to believe, are gifts of God. He concluded that Semi-Pelagianism, by attaching a small, even infinitesimally small, free will and choice to man, came down to the same thing as Pelagianism. It took away the grace of God.

Pelagianism was condemned at the ecumenical council of Ephesus in 431 AD. Pelagius has created mixed feelings in the Church till today. Two councils in Africa condemned him in 416 AD on the basis of his book on Free Will; he was excommunicated by Pope Innocent I in 417 AD, but Pope Zosimus lifted and reinstated him in 418 AD. A synod of Antioch barred him from Palestine in 424 AD. The North African bishops were always strongly behind Augustine (perhaps because he was one of them); they condemned Pelagianism. The Council of Orange gave the final condemnation of Semi-Pelagianism and endorsed Augustinian as the Western (Roman Catholic) church official doctrine. Future doctrines such as Calvinism or Arminianism were a follow up of Pelagian controversies. Calvinism was more or less Augustianism while Arminianism was a revival of Semi-Pelagianism; in other words, the debate on free will lingers on till today.

SIXTEENTH CENTURY DOCTRINES

The second stage of the Protestant Reformation was the development of doctrines of grace. There were two major doctrines of grace: Calvinism and Arminianism.

CALVINISM

Calvinism is a doctrine of salvation that bears the name of a French reformer, John Calvin (1509-1564), a theologian, who wrote a system of doctrines and practices that stemmed from his works. Calvinism is acceptable and influential among various groups in Europe. He became the most influential among reformed theologians. Calvin thought along lines linked with the theological teachings of Augustine of Hippo. Calvinism stresses the sovereignty or rule of God in all things in salvation and also in all of life. The five points of Calvinism (TULIP), serves as a summary of the differences between Calvinism and Arminianism; they were a point-by-point response to the five points of the Arminian Remonstrance's defense in 1619, written by Calvinists; Calvin himself never used the model and never challenged Arminianism directly. However, the TULIP was based on the writings and teaching of Calvin. TULIP stands for Total depravity, Unconditional election, Limited atonement, Irresistible grace, and Perseverance of the saints. The doctrine is a replica of Augustine's doctrine.

Basically, Calvinism teaches that man is totally depraved, and has no capacity to receive salvation. Those that God, in His sovereignty, has chosen to be saved will be saved by God's "irresistible grace." The "elected" cannot reject salvation. The rest of humanity, not chosen by God, has no opportunity to be saved. Calvinism teaches that Christ's death was not for all people, but only for the elect who would be saved.

> Calvinism is often called the "Doctrine of Grace" which is a contradiction, because Calvinism denies God's grace to most of mankind. – Abrams

There are several groups of Calvinists, such as, the extremist called, the "Hyper," the "Five Point", and the "Moderate" Calvinists. The Hyper and Five Point Calvinists hold to the 5-Point Calvinism. The Moderate Calvinists do not accept all of these five points, rejecting the Hyper or Five Point Calvinistic teaching of "Limited Atonement".

There are many strong objections to Calvinism. The main one is the *doctrine of double predestination.* Simply stated, this doctrine claims that God predestined or elected some to be saved and others to be lost. Those elected to salvation are decreed by God to receive salvation and cannot "resist God's grace." However, those that God elected to be lost are born condemned eternally to the Lake of Fire and He will not allow them to be saved. Another major controversial doctrine is eternal security, popularly known as "once saved, always saved (OSAS)". This view implies that man cannot fall from grace despite apostasy or unrepentant and habitual sin; the individual is truly saved if they accepted Christ at any point in the past

ARMINIANISM

Arminianism is closely related to Calvinism and the two share many doctrines in common. However, they are viewed as rivals because of their differences over the doctrines of predestination and free will. Jacobus Arminius (1560-1609), a Dutch theologian, was a student of Theodore Beza, Calvin's successor. Arminius rejected several tenets of the Calvinist doctrines of salvation but he died before he could defend his views before a national synod. Arminianism serves as an umbrella term for doctrine devolped by both Arminius and his followers (Reformed Arminians) and the Remonstrants (who revised Arminius' doctrine). When Arminius died, the Remonstrants replied in his stead with the Five articles of Remonstrance. The Remonstrants' doctrine was rejected at the Synod of Dort (composed of mainly Calvinists) held in Dordrecht, Holland, in 1618. However, many evangelical Christians adopted the Remonstrants' doctrine. The historic debate between Calvinists and Arminians led to the emergence of new movements and heated discussions and divergence in these new movements. For example, the first Baptists in seventeenth-century England were Arminians. In 1644, the new Baptist movement, embracing strong Calvinism, was formed. Also, fellow Methodists, John Wesley and George Whitfield, differed between Arminianism and Calvinism. Wesley was a defender of Arminian teachings. He brought Arminius' system to life again during his revivals and today, it is still prominent in the Methodist movement.

Arminian has clements of Semi-Pelagian views. There are generally two variants of Arminian theology - Classical Arminianism (drawn from the teaching of Jacobus Arminius), and Wesleyan Arminian (drawn from Wesley's teachings). Arminianism and Calvinism sometimes both exist in many Protestant denominations. Both also coexist in the Anglican Communion.

NINETEENTH CENTURY DOCTRINE

Abraham Kuyper (1837-1920), a Dutch theologian, journalist, social and spiritual activist, statesman and politician, was the author of the doctrine of *common grace*. In his 1862 Doctor of Theology dissertation where he compared the views of John Calvin and the more tolerant Jan Łaski, Kuyper showed a clear sympathy for Łaski. A year after (1863), Kuyper became a minister of the Dutch Reformed Church in 1863 in Beesd, Netherlands; and a year after (1864), he established correspondence with Guillaume Groen van Prinsterer, also of the Reformed Church and an historic icon, who was then a Member of Parliament. In 1879, Kuyper founded the Anti-Revolutionary Party and was prime minister of the Netherlands between 1901 and 1905 (Wikipedia).

Kuyper is considered the Father of Dutch Neo-Calvinism. His active involvement in Dutch politics and church reforms helped in the development of his spiritual social reforms skills. As also discussed in "*Missional Reformation*" (Olowe 2009), Kuyper's doctrine of common grace provides a theological backbone for a Missional Church. A Missional Church is a postmodern church that is committed to the implementation of the Great Commission of Matthew 28 through cultural engagement. In his six lectures at Princeton University in 1898 under the auspices of The Stone Foundation, Kuyper defines common grace:

> Common grace is by which God maintains the life of the world, by relaxing the sins, and allows the untrammeled development of our life to glorify Himself as Creator.
>
> Common grace has led to the result that an unregenerate sinner may captivate and attract us by much that is lovely and full of energy, just as our domestic animals do, but this of course after the manner of man. The nature of sin, however, remains as venomous as it was.

Without common grace, man would not have been allowed to exist in the first place because of his sinful state; man would have been doing one evil after another. He particularly covered application of Calvinism in four areas of life (www.lgmarshall.org):

1. Religion
2. Politics (State)
3. Science
4. Art

Although he wrote about applying Calvinism in these four spheres, Kuyper actually recognizes that there are other spheres from this statement:

> In a Calvinistic sense we understand hereby, that the family, the business, science, art and so forth are all social spheres, which do not owe their existence to the state, and which do not derive the law of their life from the superiority of the state, but obey a high authority within their own bosom; an authority which rules, by the grace of God, just as the sovereignty of the State does.

Kuyper teaches that all human, whether saved or not, receives common grace as part of God's purpose to build His Kingdom. Kuyper notes that if God is Sovereign, then his Lordship must remain over all life and cannot be closed up within church walls. The secular world has not been given over to satan or to fallen humanity. Man is required to make use of the common grace to perform his stewardship duty. Kuyper's Calvinism tendency influences his political views. For example, Kuyper shows support for capital punishment since God decreed it in the Old Testament.

In this study, it is realized that the common or universal grace extends beyond divine grace to man, it also includes material gifts. The term "universal" describes best this kind of grace rather than "common". Universal grace will be adopted as the correct term for this grace. In this book, we will provide a deeper insight on universal grace and use many of Kuyper's arguments to support our future discussion.

Reformed theologians are divided on the common grace doctrine. While some churches adopt it, others reject the doctrine. Professor Herman Hanko, a Reformed theologian, has written, on his blog, several articles on the doctrine of common grace.

2. MERCY AND GRACE

MERCY and grace are two attributes of God that can be confused to mean the same by lay people. But there is a difference. On answers.yahoo.com, a blogger puts it this way:

> The belief that grace and mercy are near synonyms, almost interchangeable concepts, is a gross misunderstanding by many. So much of Christianity thinks of grace as a kind of blanket mercy which is constantly forgiving all sin and cancels out the Law of God. Many have believed the error that grace allows them to disobey God's Law; that since grace abounds, sin may abound without penalty. This is especially taught by those who wish to ignore the eternal Law of God, or certain parts of it. Such doctrine is a nearly fatal error, because it waters down God's righteousness and calls into question His eternal faithfulness. It also misconstrues His kindness, and many have gone

> astray and departed from the truth because of this misinformation.

MERCY

> O give thanks unto the Lord: for He is good, for His mercy endureth forever Ps. 136:1.

The Psalmist, in as many verses in Ps. 106, 107, 118, and 136, repeatedly times and times over, calls us to give thanks unto the Lord for His mercy. And surely, when we reflect on this adorable attribute of God, we cannot do otherwise than bless His Divine Excellency for it.

So what is mercy? Mercy has been defined as "feeling sympathy with the misery of another, and especially sympathy manifested in act" (Vine).

> Mercy is more than just sympathetic feelings. It is sympathy in concert with action. (Bert Thompson)

Mercy is applied in two slightly different contexts, for help and for pardon.

MERCY FOR PARDON

The most understood and talked about is when mercy is used in the context of forgiveness or sin relaxation. In this case, justice is ignored. Mercy is giving for forgiveness, out of compassion, to relax punishment. It is a disposition to pardon the guilty. Its exercise consists in arresting and setting aside the penalty of law, when that penalty has been incurred by transgression. It is, as has been said, directly opposed to justice. In this context, mercy is exercised only where there is guilt. The penalty of the law must have been previously incurred; else there can be no scope for mercy.

> And there shall cleave nought of the cursed thing to thine hand: that the Lord may turn from the fierceness of his anger, and shew thee mercy, and have compassion upon thee, and multiply thee, as he hath sworn unto thy fathers; Deut. 13:17

> Have mercy upon me, O God, according to thy lovingkindness: according unto the multitude of thy tender mercies blot out my transgressions. Ps. 51:1

> And I will strengthen the house of Judah, and I will save the house of Joseph, and I will bring them again to place them; for I have mercy upon them: and they shall be as though I had not cast them off: for I am the Lord their God, and will hear them. Zech. 10: 6

> But go ye and learn what that meaneth, I WILL HAVE MERCY, AND NOT SACRIFICE: for I am not come to call the righteous, but sinners to repentance. Matt. 9:13

> He that covereth his sins shall not prosper: but whoso confesseth and forsaketh them shall have mercy.
> Prov. 28:13

MERCY FOR HELP

Secondly, mercy is applied as compassion toward the afflicted, the helpless, and to provide help to someone who needs to get out of misery. The misery may not necessarily be because of sin, although Jesus shows in Matt. 9 that sometimes sickness is due to sin. The one who is merciful must have the authority and ability to provide the needed help.

> Have mercy upon me, O Lord; for I am weak: O Lord, heal me; for my bones are vexed. Ps. 6: 2

> Withhold not good from them to whom it is due, when it is in the power of thine hand to do it. Say not unto thy neighbour, Go, and come again, and to morrow I will give; when thou hast it by thee" (Prov. 3:27-28)

> Hear, O Lord, and have mercy upon me: Lord, be thou my helper. Ps. 30: 10

> And when Jesus departed thence, two blind men followed him, crying, and saying, Thou Son of David, have mercy on us. Matt. 9: 27

> And, behold, a woman of Canaan came out of the same coasts, and cried unto him, saying, Have mercy on me, O Lord, thou Son of David; my daughter is grievously vexed with a devil. Matt. 15: 22

> And as he entered into a certain village, there met him ten men that were lepers, which stood afar off: And they lifted up their voices, and said, Jesus, Master, have mercy on us. Luke 17: 12-13

Some cases of help may still be linked with forgiveness. In the case of the man sick of palsy (Matt. 9), having healing mercy on him was done by relaxing sin. Jesus asked:

> For whether is easier, to say, Thy sins be forgiven thee; or to say, Arise, and walk? Matt. 9:5

GRACE

A common phrase we often use all the time is "by the grace of God". We find this in the scripture several times. In Paul's epistles (for example 1 Cor. 15:10), he uses it often. The grace in some of these phrases is not referring to the grace of salvation, but it is a way of seeking the favor of God. So, God's favor is a grace. The grace of God comes is several forms. In the Old Testament (OT), the word "grace" appears in 37 verses and most of the usages signify "favor". In the New Testament (NT), the word "grace" appears in 122 verses and the focus is on the saving grace of God through Christ. God's grace is a free gift from Him (Rom. 5:15). More importantly, this gift is unmerited; as such, it remains within God's sovereign right to bestow it as He sees fit. Several believers have perceived the existence of the two kinds of grace from God, universal grace (for everyone) and special grace (for believers), but our existing doctrines of grace have limited the usage of grace to salvation alone. The Catholic theologians define grace as follows:

> Grace (gratia, Charis), in general, is a supernatural gift of God to intellectual creatures (men, angels) for their eternal salvation, whether the latter be furthered and attained through salutary acts or a state of holiness. (newadvent.org)

Although the Catholic theologians also define actual grace and sanctifying grace, but they are in the context of salvation only. Many other believers understand grace as a gift from God, but also limit grace to salvation. A blogger (askville.amazon.com) threw out a question: "What does Grace mean to you?" Here are some anonymous responses:

> We were taught that grace stood for "God's Riches at Christ's Expense." The Lutheran church I grew up in was very kind and forgiving and I never understood grace as anything other than a free gift.
>
> Grace is a supernatural gift of God to mankind for their eternal salvation, whether the latter be furthered and attained through salutary acts or a state of holiness. Grace is indispensable and Divinely ordained, to effect the redemption from sin through Christ and to lead men to their eternal destiny in Heaven. Through the grace of God we are able to attain justification through faith and acts of goodness and piety.
>
> Grace is basically a gift. It does not come as a result of something a person did or in recognition of an accomplishment or milestone. So, unlike a birthday or Christmas gift that one receives in recognition of an event, grace is given to us by God for no reason. All of us are recipients of the grace of God regardless of how "good" or "bad" we are.

SCOPE OF GRACE

Even though Salvation is the greatest gift God has given to us, it is not the only gift we receive from God. The Grace of God is unlimited and infinite. When other believers speak about grace, they cut across both universal grace and special grace, all lumped in one. Here are some quotations from various sources:

> Like any other gift, the gift of grace can be yours only if you'll reach out and take it. Maybe being able to reach out and take it is a gift too. -- Rev. Margaret Gunness

> More broadly, divine grace refers to God's gifts to humankind, including life, creation, and salvation. More narrowly but more commonly, grace describes the means by which humans are saved from original sin and granted salvation. This latter concept of grace is of central importance in the theology of Christianity, as well as one of the most contentious issues in Christian sectarianism. - Wikipedia

> Grace is enabling power sufficient for progression. Grace divine is an indispensable gift from God for development, improvement, and character expansion. Without God's grace, there are certain limitations, weaknesses, flaws, impurities, and faults (i.e. carnality) humankind cannot overcome. Therefore, it is necessary to increase in God's grace for added perfection, completeness, and flawlessness. (qna.rediff.com)(divinegraceoutreach.org)

> Divine grace refers to God's gifts to all mankind, including life. (qna.rediff.com)

All the above quotations talk about both the universal grace and the special grace. Gifts of life, character expansion, the earth, and so on are all from the universal grace of God. The Old Testament use of grace is more of the universal kind. In the New Testament, the focus is more on the special grace.

PURPOSE OF GRACE OF GOD

God's grace preserves life.

> But Noah found grace in the eyes of the Lord (Gen 6: 8)
>
> Behold, now thy servant hath found grace in thy sight, and thou hast magnified thy mercy, which thou hast shewed unto me in saving my life; and I cannot escape to the mountain, lest some evil take me, and I die.
> Gen. 19:19

God's Grace enables us to manage His affairs and do good works.

> For we are his workmanship, created in Christ Jesus unto good works, which God hath before ordained that we should walk in them. Eph. 2: 10
>
> And God is able to make all grace abound toward you; that ye, always having all sufficiency in all things, may abound to every good work: 2 Cor. 9: 8

God's Grace offers us salvation.

> For by grace are ye saved through faith; and that not of yourselves: it is the gift of God: Eph. 2: 8

For the grace of God that bringeth salvation hath appeared to all men Tit. 2: 11

Of which salvation the prophets have enquired and searched diligently, who prophesied of the grace that should come unto you: 1 Pet. 1: 10

God's Grace offers us forgiveness of sins.

In whom we have redemption through his blood, the forgiveness of sins, according to the riches of his grace; Eph. 1: 7

God's Grace offers us fellowship with God.

Therefore being justified by faith, we have peace with God through our Lord Jesus Christ: By whom also we have access by faith into this grace wherein we stand, and rejoice in hope of the glory of God. Rom. 5: 1-2

God's Grace offers us riches of the earth and wisdom.

So king Solomon exceeded all the kings of the earth for riches and for wisdom. 1 Kings 10: 23

O Lord, how manifold are thy works! in wisdom hast thou made them all: the earth is full of thy riches.
Ps. 104: 24

When thy wares went forth out of the seas, thou filledst many people; thou didst enrich the kings of the earth with the multitude of thy riches and of thy merchandise.
Eze. 27: 33

God's Grace offers us Spiritual blessings.

> Having then gifts differing according to the grace that is given to us, whether prophecy, let us prophesy according to the proportion of faith; Rom. 12: 6

God's Grace offers eternal life.

> That as sin hath reigned unto death, even so might grace reign through righteousness unto eternal life by Jesus Christ our Lord. Rom. 5: 21

> That being justified by his grace, we should be made heirs according to the hope of eternal life. Tit. 3: 7

Who can search his life and honestly say he deserves such blessings as these? Yet God offers them anyway. That is "unmerited favor." All manifestations of grace will be discussed in Chapter 3.

DIFFERENCES BETWEEN MERCY AND GRACE

> I will make all My goodness pass before thee, and I will proclaim the name of the Lord before thee; and will be gracious to whom I will be gracious, and will show mercy on whom I will show mercy (Ex. 33:19).

This passage shows that there is a basic difference between the mercy and the grace of God. The basic difference is that grace is a *gift* not deserved while mercy is a *pardon (clem-*

ency) not deserved. Mercy is one attribute while grace comes in several forms; there are different kinds of gifts.

Many describc thc difference between mercy and grace (in relation to salvation) in the following terms:

> Grace is receiving what you don't deserve (unmerited favor); while Mercy is not receiving what you deserve (withheld punishment).

Mercy is like a court finding you guilty, but then withholding any punishment. Grace is getting something you could never have imagined, an inexplicable gift. It is like the same judge awarding you $10 million, after finding you guilty.

One other basic difference is that, in the Old Testament, mercy of God was needed for salvation.

> But I have trusted in thy mercy; my heart shall rejoice in thy salvation. Ps. 13: 5

> Shew us thy mercy, O Lord, and grant us thy salvation. Ps. 85: 7

When Jesus died for mankind, the mercy for salvation is replaced with *special grace*. Mercy is then limited for other things besides salvation.

> For the law was given by Moses, but grace and truth came by Jesus Christ. John 1: 17

Grace is a potential made available to mankind for use. A potential remains a potential until it is used. Gift of salvation is a potential available to everyone. We no longer need to pray directly to God for salvation. The grace is available for us to use. Instead of asking for mercy for grace, we only need to ask for God's guidance to receive those things that are already.

3. MANIFESTATIONS OF GRACE

GRACE has been defined as an unmerited gift of God in form of potential or resource. In this Chapter, we will examine the various kinds of gifts and how God intends us to use them. God's grace is upon all humanity. Our gifts are our potentials. All mankind have access to these potentials. In this context, gift and grace can be used interchangeably.

CLASSIFICATION OF GRACE

As we have read in the previous Chapter, God's grace is infinite and comes in several forms. However, God's grace can be classified under two broad categories:

- o Universal Grace that is used by all humanity (believers and unbelievers);
- o Special Grace that is used by only believers.

Both Universal Grace and Special Grace are available to all humanity.

For over 1500 years now, the Church has been debating over the issue of grace (special) and good works, especially on Justification. The discussion on justification will be covered in Chapter 7. Equating salvation to faith and works has been the fundamental error. This is discussed in *Missional Reformation* (Olowe 2009).

SPECIAL GRACE

The propitiation with the blood of Jesus is the source of the special grace of God.

> In whom we have redemption through his blood, the forgiveness of sins, according to the riches of his grace; Eph. 1: 7

> Even when we were dead in sins, hath quickened us together with Christ, (by grace ye are saved;) Eph. 2: 5

This special grace is available to all mankind and it is received by those who believe in the Faith.

UNIVERSAL GRACE

We have to acknowledge Abraham Kuyper as the first person to elaborate on universal grace, that he called "common grace".

> For not only did God create all men, not only is He all for all men, but His grace also extends itself, not only as a special grace, to the elect, but also as a common grace (gratia communis) to all mankind (Kuyper)

However, the scope of the grace is extended here and it is preferably called "universal grace". It is surprising that Kuyper remained a Calvinist and defended its theology. A synopsis of Kuyper's doctrine of common or universal grace has been stated in Chapter 1. Kuyper regarded every sector of the society, such as, education, business, law, politics, and so on, as all unholy. Kuyper explained that every sector (sphere) of the society is sinful and it is the duty of Christians to reconcile these spheres to God.

> What follows from this is Christian responsibility for engagement in every area of life.
>
> Thus the church receded in order to be neither more or less than the congregation of believers, and in every department the life of the world was not emancipated from God, but from the dominion of the Church. Thus domestic life regained its independence, trade and commerce realized their strength in liberty, art and science

> were set free from every ecclesiastical bond and restored to their own inspirations, and man began to understand the subjection of all nature with its hidden forces and treasures to himself as a holy duty, imposed upon him by the original ordinances of Paradise: "Have dominion over them". Henceforth the curse should no longer rest upon the world itself, but upon that which is sinful in it, and instead of monastic flight from the world the duty is now emphasized of serving God in the world, in every position in life. (Kuyper)

Kuyper explains universal (common) grace as follows:

> God arrested sin in its course in order to prevent the complete annihilation of His divine handiwork, which naturally would have followed. He has interfered in the life of the individual, in the life of mankind as a whole, and in the life of nature itself by His common grace. This grace, however, does not kill the core of sin, nor does it save unto life eternal, but it arrests the complete effectuation of sin, just as human insight arrests the fury of wild beasts.
>
> There is a particular grace which works Salvation, and also a common grace by which God, maintaining the life of the world, relaxes the curse which rests upon it, arrests its process of corruption, and thus allows the untrammeled development of our life in which to glorify Himself as Creator

From the above statements, Kuyper postulates that universal grace of God provides support in three areas:

1. God's grace to all mankind to preserve life;
2. God's grace to all mankind to assist in making right choices, including salvation;

3. imparting Christian values in different spheres of the society; this becomes useful in discipling in specific sectors rather than global evangelism;

Universal grace extends beyond these three areas. The gift of the Earth and its riches are part of the grace. Also, human virtues and some characteristic elements are part of the universal grace. They are given to all humanity.

> It is common grace which makes special grace possible, prepares the way for it, and later supports it; and special grace, in its turn, leads common grace up to its own level and puts it into its service. (Herman Bavinck)

Theologians in defense of "common grace" have used Matthew 5:45-46 as strong evidence in support of its existence:

> Love your enemies, bless them that curse you, do good to them that hate you, and pray for them which despitefully use you, and persecute you; That ye may be the children of your Father which is in Heaven: for he maketh his sun to rise on the evil and on the good, and sendeth rain on the just and on the unjust.
> Matt. 5:44-45

God, by His universal grace, sends rain to the just and the unjust and He is asking the just to love everyone.

William Masselink wrote extensively on "general revelation" as a common grace of God in a book under the title, *General Revelation and Common Grace.* He argues that God's revelation of Himself in creation and history constitutes in itself the common grace of God. Other theologians have used this "general revelation" theory to explain some miracles and even the age of the earth. The validity of such arguments can not be verified in this book. Professor Hanko (October 2009) have written extensively on "general revelation". Although Professor Hanko, a Reformed Faith theologian, thinks that the whole concept of "general revelation" should be abandoned, there are still valid arguments, such as the explanation of divine restraint (covered below), that still leaves the door opened for further exploration. Hanko says:

> It is difficult, if not impossible, to imagine how God can be gracious in the sense of being favorably inclined to someone while he is not also gracious towards someone in saving him. (Hanko, April 2009)

Yes, God tries to save everyone through the universal grace. This will further be discussed in this book.

GIFTS

As highlighted in Chapter 2, grace of God is a gift from God. We are going to show all manifestations of the grace of God in form of gifts. There are five forms of gifts God has given us by His grace; two come from special grace and three from universal grace. They are:

<u>Universal Grace</u>: material universal gifts, divine universal gifts, and spiritual universal gifts;

<u>Special Grace</u>: divine special gift and spiritual special gifts.

Time is included in the material universal gift. All gifts can be classified under two categories: *intrinsic* (or innate) gifts and *extrinsic* (or obtained) gifts (corresponding to intrinsic grace and extrinsic grace respectively). An intrinsic gift (or grace) is what is given to man before his birth. The term "extrinsic" does not mean it is obtained because of good works of man, it is just a qualifier. Grace is not usually given as a result of any good works of man (Eph. 2:8-9). By virtue of being made available, grace is irresistible. The term "irresistible" in this context means you cannot say "I don't want it". However, the question is in the response coming from the Will of man. With exception of divine grace (see below), other forms of grace may be ignored or disregarded, which means the Will can say "No, but thanks. I don't need it". Will may not respond to grace and make a wrong choice.

MATERIAL UNIVERSAL GRACE

Material gifts are gifts of time, the Earth, and all of its resources and riches, including, the air, the sea, animals, minerals, plants, rain, snow, and so on. So, they are from universal grace and belong to *intrinsic gifts* category because they exist before man is born whether he likes it or not.

> Every man also to whom God hath given riches and wealth, and hath given him power to eat thereof, and to take his portion, and to rejoice in his labour; this is the gift of God. Eccl 5:19

The Owner

God the Creator is the owner of the earth and all its resources

> God created the Heavens and the earth (Gen. 1:1) and created man in His own image (Gen. 1:26).
>
> For all that is in the Heaven and in the earth is thine (1 Chr. 29:11); The earth is the Lord's, and everything in it, the world, and all who live in it (Ps. 24:1, 89:11); The earth is full of thy riches (Ps. 104:24); He giveth to all life, and breath, and all things (Acts 17:25); the silver is Mine, and the gold is Mine (Hag. 2:8); every beast of the forest is Mine, and the cattle upon a thousand hills (Ps. 50:10).

But He graciously allows all men to use them.

> He gives men power to get wealth (Deut. 8:18).
>
> Moreover the profit of the earth is for all: the king himself is served by the field. Eccl. 5:9

Role of man

Men are managers for Him.

> The Lord God took the man and put him in the Garden of Eden to work it and take care of it. (Gen. 2:15)
>
> Thou madest him to have dominion over the works of thy hands; thou hast put all things under his feet. (Ps 8:6)

Gift of Time

God is gracious to man with time. There are several phrases being used with time that portrays time as a material gift, such as "time is precious", "time is money", "quality time", and "time flies". The fact that God created the sun, the moon, and the stars to mark time, indicates that God controls time. A Pastor asks:

> Why does God give one person so much time on earth even when they are in pain, even when they are ready to "go home" to their Lord, even more time than the person perhaps wants--and yet another dies after ten brief years of life? (DeVries)

God exists outside of time, but He created time for us. He has numbered our days and given us opportunity to fulfill His plan during our lives.

> So teach us to number our days, that we may apply our hearts unto wisdom. Ps 90:12

Also, the fact that the earth rotates about its axis for 24 hours and around the sun for 1 year in an endless loop, makes time itself to be infinite. God gives us time to repent (He is slow to anger), He gives us time to fellowship with Him, He gives us time for whatever we need to do. God gives us time for us to use wisely, but we sometimes squander it. Each time that passes cannot be recovered. Some need more than the 24 hours of a day to meet all their commitments that demand precious time. With time, we learn many lessons, build experience, and heal many wounds. What does the scripture say about the allocation of time?

Time is scheduled for a purpose

> I said in mine heart, God shall judge the righteous and the wicked: for there is a time there for every purpose and for every work. Eccl 3: 17

> And, behold, they cried out, saying, What have we to do with thee, Jesus, thou Son of God? art thou come hither to torment us before the time? Matt 8: 29

Time is scheduled for a fulfillment

> And saying, The time is fulfilled, and the Kingdom of God is at hand: repent ye, and believe the Gospel. Mark 1:15

> Now my soul troubled; and what shall I say? Father, save me from this hour: but for this cause came I unto this hour. John 12:27

> But when the fulness of the time was come, God sent forth his Son, made of a woman, made under the law, Gal 4:4

> For Sarah conceived, and bare Abraham a son in his old age, at the set time of which God had spoken to him. Gen 21:2

Time is seasonal

> To every thing there is a season, and a time to every purpose under the Heaven ... Eccl 3:1-14

To everything there is a time.

> I returned, and saw under the sun, that the race is not to the swift, nor the battle to the strong, neither yet bread to the wise, nor yet riches to men of skill; but time and chance happeneth to them all. Eccl 9:11

SPIRITUAL UNIVERSAL GRACE

As will be discussed at length in Chapter 4, the spiritual universal gifts reside in the soul of man. They are potentials made available, through the good elements to preserve life and to assist the soul in making good decisions. As will be discussed in Chapter 4, there are millions of these elements (gifts). The spiritual universal gifts shape the virtues and values of man. The main purpose of spiritual universal gifts (or universal grace in general) is to enable man to succumb to the Will of God – to succumb to salvation and to do good works. It is by the universal grace that these gifts are made available to believers and non believers alike. Some universal gifts are intrinsic and some are extrinsic. We shall discuss a few specific ones.

Gift of Life

The gift of life is the only gift that is both irresistible and cannot be disregarded; that means it requires a positive response (right choice). All other gifts are irresistible but do not require the right choice. The gift of life preserves the life of the soul and body of man.

> God arrested sin in its course in order to prevent the complete annihilation of His divine handiwork, which naturally would have followed. He has interfered in the life of the individual, in the life of mankind as a whole, and in the life of nature itself by His common grace. This grace, however, does not kill the core of sin, nor does it save unto life eternal, but it arrests the complete effectuation of sin, just as human insight arrests the fury of wild beasts. (Kuyper)

Note that man can still respond negatively to the gift of life by taking his own life, but then, he doesn't exist anymore and there will be no point talking about the gift. The gift is for life preservation and not for eternal life. Eternal life can only be obtained through initial salvation and good works (see discussion on Justification in Chapter 9):

> For the wages of sin is death; but the gift of God is eternal life through Jesus Christ our Lord. (Rom. 6:23)

Gift of Repentance

To repent and obtain the special grace is a gift. Many disregard it and some respond positively to it. This gift complements the remorse element (Chapter 4).

> Remorse is an emotional expression of personal regret felt by a person after he or she has committed an act which they deem to be shameful, hurtful, or violent. - Wikipedia

Gift of Talent

Skill is a term that relates to talent but it is not a gift; skill is developed. Skill is the expertise one develops by himself through learning. Through universal grace, God endows individuals with the gift of talent within a particular sphere, according to His purpose for us; for example, Bazeleel received his in Arts and Science spheres.

> And I have filled him with the spirit of God, in wisdom, and in understanding, and in knowledge, and in all manner of workmanship, to devise cunning works, to work in gold, and in silver, and in brass, and in cutting of stones, to set them, and in carving of timber, to work in all manner of workmanship. (Exo. 31: 3-5)

Talent is usually an *intrinsic gift* but the above example shows that it can also be *extrinsic* in emergency situations or perhaps through prayers.

> All Christians are called to develop God-given talents, to make the most of their lives, to develop to the fullest their God-given powers and capacities. (Oswald Sanders)

Gift of Destiny

Definitely, destiny is an *intrinsic* universal grace of God and it is given to all mankind. God gives each man gift of talents to succeed (Jer. 29:11). Every man has a purpose of creation and an assignment to carry out. Destiny is what some call "the Will of God for my life". The issue of "predestination" comes in here. There is no such thing as salvation before birth; it diminishes the importance of the blood Jesus shed. You have to be born to know what Jesus did and then accept him. It is true that some people may be destined to work in the service of the Lord (Jer. 1:5); that is *preordination* and it does not translate to salvation. No salvation is received before birth. The gift of salvation is extrinsic and it is available to all mankind; those who respond to the urging of the Holy Spirit through the universal grace obtain the special grace and hence salvation. Destiny is an offer made in a contract; it is not valid until positively responded to. Destiny like other intrinsic gifts cannot be resisted but may be ignored. Man does not have any ability to alter destiny, or any grace for that matter, except the Creator; however, man may not reach or deviate from his destiny if he does not respond to the grace. Your talent or preordination is God's gift to take you to your promised land, your destiny, for your prosperity and fulfillment, if used according to His purpose.

> Nothing is worse on earth than death of a dream (Myles Munroe)

> The wealthiest spot on earth is the cemetery; there is filled with books that were never written, ministries that never started, music that was never played, poetry that was never read – that wealth is called potential (Myles Munroe)

Gift of Conscience

Conscience is a gift of the Mind that urges the corrupted Will of man to make the right choice. When it is said that some-one has no conscience, it simply means that his Will does not respond to urging and can therefore not make the right choice. Thomas Aquinas in *Summa Theologica* writes thus:

> If obeying and disobeying a mistaken conscience are both bad, it seems that men with mistaken consciences are caught in a trap, and cannot avoid sin.

Here is a dictionary definition of conscience:

> The sense of what is right and wrong that governs some-body's thoughts and actions, urging him or her to do right rather than wrong (Encarta)

From the definition, "right and wrong" is from the Will, "thought" is from the Mind and "actions" is body's response. The process of salvation could be said to start from the Holy Spirit urging the conscience to remorse, then to repentance. It is this process that draws man to God. Jesus said:

> No man can come to me, except the Father which hath sent me draw him: and I will raise him up at the last day. John 6:44

Here is the interpretation of the above scripture by the Application Study Bible:

> God, not man, plays the most active role in salvation. When someone chooses to believe in Jesus Christ as Savior, he does so only in response to the urging of the Holy Spirit. God does the urging; then we decide whether or not to believe. Thus no one can believe in Jesus without God's help.

The Will of man can either respond to the urging or not to make the right choice. Will of man is covered in Chapter 4.

Other Gifts

The ability of man to possess positive qualities (virtues and values) such as kindness, honesty, sincerity, compassion, wisdom, meekness, and so on, comes from the spiritual universal gifts. Gifts such as help, wisdom, giving, showing mercy, and leadership, listed by Paul as special gifts in the Bible, may be counted as universal gifts; this will further be discussed under spiritual special gifts below. There are philanthropists who are not believers. Spiritual universal gifts can be intrinsic or extrinsic, and some such as wisdom (as in the case of Bezaleel and Solomon) are both intrinsic and extrinsic. This area is complex and needs more work as the number of gifts is inexhaustible; also, we need to draw the line between spiritual gifts obtained through special grace and those obtained through universal grace (that is, the ones that reside in the soul and the ones in the spiritual frame (Chapter 4)); sometimes, there is a mix up.

DIVINE UNIVERSAL GRACE

Divine universal gifts are external gifts from God; this means that they do not reside in man and they are not resources used by man to accomplish good works (see Chapter 4 and "*Missional Reformation*" (Olowe 2009). They are the working of the Holy Spirit to assist man (believer or unbeliever) in certain situations. They are also simply called *divine grace*. It is a way of God keeping a watchful eye on man; when man runs into a difficult situation beyond which soul can make a rightful decision, God intervenes through His divine grace to help. Divine grace is the basis of Kuyper's doctrine of common grace. Divine grace stems from the attributes of God: mercy, goodness, wrath, compassion, forgiveness, and so on. Divine grace can generally be classified into two kinds: *favor* (with a positive connotation) and *restraint* (with a negative connotation).

Divine Favor

This is a positive grace of God towards mankind irrespective of salvation. It is an *extrinsic* universal grace. We find various passages where unregenerate men are recipients of divine favor. The Lord blessed the Egyptian's house for Joseph's sake.

> And it came to pass from the time that he had made him overseer in his house, and over all that he had, that the LORD blessed the Egyptian's house for Joseph's sake; and the blessing of the LORD was upon all that he had in the house, and in the field. Gen 39: 5

Laban was blessed for Jacob's sake.

> And Laban said unto him, I pray thee, if I have found favour in thine eyes, tarry: for I have learned by experience that the LORD hath blessed me for thy sake. Gen 30: 27

So, not only the believers receive God's favor. There are also cases of fatal accidents where one can miraculously escape death. Divine favor is in two forms:

1. Direct favor to man through blessings;
2. Indirect favor to man through restraint of a calamity.

The second form will be discussed further under "restraint".

Divine Restraint

Divine restraint, an *extrinsic* universal grace, is seen as opposite of divine favor; it is therefore seen in a negative sense, but it is still granted to assist man. The Holy Spirit serves as the agent that communicates the fear of God into man.

> By the fear of the Lord men depart from evil. Prov. 16: 6

Without divine restraint, man's life would consist of one evil act after another. Divine restraint prevents man from thwarting God's purpose.

> It is God's common grace that prevents man from following the desires of his heart without restraint (Bacote).

> Common grace restrains the operation of sin in man, partly by breaking its power, partly by taming his evil spirit, and partly by domesticating his nation or his family (Kuyper).

William Masselink demonstrated a connection between "general revelation" and divine restraint in his book, entitled *General Revelation and Common Grace*. He says:

> They are related, however, because in common grace God uses the truths of general revelation to restrain sin. The two results of general revelation are: God-consciousness and moral consciousness. By means of these two results, through God's common grace, sin is curbed in the natural man.

Divine restraint manifests in two forms:

1. Directly applied to a man from sinning to God.
2. Applied to a situation, another person, or the enemy, on behalf of a man to prevent calamity.

The second form is actually an indirect divine favor to the first man; as in mathematics, a negative of a negative is positive. In the passage below, God restrained king Abimelech of Gerar from messing with Abraham's wife.

> And God said unto him in a dream, Yea, I know that thou didst this in the integrity of thy heart; for I also withheld thee from sinning against Me. (Gen. 20:6)

DIVINE SPECIAL GRACE

The only divine special gift is gift of salvation. This gift is received through special grace. The gift of salvation is made available to all mankind. Those who believe in Jesus Christ, in their heart, as savior are able to obtain this gift through the working of the universal grace. Salvation is *extrinsic* whether preordained or not and it usually comes through the universal gift of repentance that assists in receiving the special grace.

> For by grace are ye saved through faith; and not of yourselves: it is the gift of God: not of works, lest any man should boast. Eph. 2:8-9

Salvation is a very powerful gift. It redefines man, connects man to Heaven, and paves the way for spiritual special gifts with which man can receive "all power in Heaven and on earth" (Matt 28:18).

SPIRITUAL SPECIAL GRACE

Spiritual special gifts are *extrinsic* special grace received by the believer; they are simply called spiritual gifts in the scripture:

> Blessed be the God and Father of our Lord Jesus Christ, who hath blessed us with all spiritual blessings in Heavenly places in Christ: Eph. 1: 3

Spiritual special gifts are given to empower believers according to their measure of faith (Rom. 12:3) and for the building of the Body of Christ, the Church. There are four lists of spiritual gifts mentioned in the epistles of Paul.

1. Rom. 12:3-8 lists: prophecy, ministering, teaching, exhorting, giving, leadership, and showing mercy.

2. 1 Cor. 12:8-10 lists: Wisdom, knowledge, faith, healing, working of miracles, prophecy, discerning of spirits, tongues, and interpretation of tongues.
3. Eph. 4:10-11 lists (offices): apostles, prophets, evangelists, and pastor-teachers.
4. 1 Cor. 12:28 lists: apostles, teachers, miracles, healing, helps, governments, tongues.

The last one has some repetitions.

Jesus has given us all power on earth and in Heaven (Matt. 28:18). Here are the powers He gives to us to carry out His commission (in the gift of working miracles):

- Power against the devil (Matt 10:1; Luke 9:1)
- Power to cast out unclean spirit (Matt 10:1, 8)
- Power to tread over serpents and scorpions (Luke 10:19)
- Power to heal (Matt 10:1, 8; Luke 9:2)
- Power to raise the dead (Matt 10:8)

Paul's lists are mere examples of spiritual gifts and he has lumped both universal and special gifts together; gifts such as helps, knowledge, wisdom, giving, and leadership are available through universal grace. As we shall see in Chapter 4, knowledge and wisdom elements reside in the soul and not in the spiritual frame; only spiritual special gifts reside in the spiritual frame of man. Everyone (believer or non believer) is given the gift of wisdom and of knowledge. However, a believer's wisdom can be improved through the Holy Spirit that resides in the heart. Also, it is suggested that the biblical lists of spiritual special gifts are not exhaustive; that there are additional ones, such as laying on of hands (Act 8:17-20) and special revelation (Matt. 11:27; 13:11), not listed by Paul. Augustine, suggested that the very beginning of faith, even the thinking and willing to believe, are gifts of God, and are not to be separated from the rest of God's gifts. Augustine's example is a universal gift discussed above.

PURPOSE OF GIFTS

Of all the five forms of gifts, it is only the divine universal grace that is not made available to man at any time; that is, it is arbitrary. Other types of grace are potentials (or resources) made available by God to mankind; until it is used, a gift remains a potential. The purpose of God's gifts is the same as explained in Chapter 4 for the purpose God gave Adam Will. There are two reasons, to have good relationship with God and to have good relationship with the environment. So that at the end, God will be appreciated and glorified for His good work (Gen. 1:31).

Man is expected to use the universal grace for his benefit and to profit others. When utilized with special grace, universal grace produces good works to the glory of God. Universal grace is available to us and if we are able to make use of it fruitfully, that justifies us of works, the second part of the Gospel of the Kingdom of God.

MATERIAL GIFTS

We need to be stewards of God's material gifts. Stewardship is defined as (Olowe 2009):

> The management of resources God has given to us.

Stewardship means:

1. To manage His affairs on earth:

> For we are His workmanship, created in Christ Jesus unto good works, which God hath before ordained that we should walk in them. Eph. 2:10

2. To take dominion

> So God created man in His own image, in the image of God created He him; male and female created he them. And God blessed them, and God said unto them, be fruitful, and multiply, and replenish the earth, and subdue it: and have dominion over the fish of the sea, and over the fowl of the air, and over every living thing that moveth upon the earth (Gen. 1:27-28)

The psalmist in the passage below cannot understand why God gives man this so much honor in spite of his sinful state.

> What is man, that thou art mindful of him? And the son of man that thou visited him? For thou hast made him a little lower than the angels, and hast crowned him with glory and honour. Thou madest him to have dominion over the works of thy hands; thou hast put all things under his feet: Psalm 8: 4-6

SPIRITUAL UNIVERSAL GIFTS

Out of gratitude for the free gifts, we should help and serve others. God gives us talent for the benefit of others.

> As every man hath received the gift, even so minister the same one to another, as good stewards of the manifold grace of God. (1 Pet. 4:10)

Productivity and fulfilling God's purpose is the ultimate goal of the material and personal resources we receive from God.

> Not because I desire a gift: but I desire fruit that may abound to your account. – Philippians 4:17

> And let ours also learn to maintain good works for necessary uses, that they be not unfruitful. – Titus 3:14

> That ye might walk worthy of the Lord unto all pleasing, being fruitful in every good work, and increasing in the knowledge of God; Colossians 1:10

GIFT OF SALVATION

The gift of salvation is needed to implement the Great Commission. Without salvation you can not make disciples. However, without salvation, man can still implement some other good works through the universal grace.

SPIRITUAL SPECIAL GIFTS

Spiritual gifts assist the intrinsic spirit of man in fellowshipping with God and in doing good works. Spiritual gifts are also needed for personal spiritual growth and to complement other believers in the Body of Christ (1 Cor. 12:12-31).

SUMMARY OF GIFTS

All the kinds of gifts discussed in this Chapter are summarized in the Table below. The gifts are either available personally to each person or available generally to everyone.

Table 3.1: Classification of Grace

	Special Grace	**Universal Grace**
Personal	Divine Special Grace, Spiritual Special Gifts	Spiritual Universal Gifts
General		Divine Universal Grace, Material Universal Gifts
Availability	To all mankind but used by the believer	To all mankind
Purpose	Salvation, fellowship with God, good works	life preservation, repentance, works, good works

Notes:

- A gift is also a grace.
- Sometimes, some spiritual universal gifts are mistaken for spiritual special gifts.
- All graces are irresistible. All may be ignored except divine universal grace and the gift of life.

4. MAN

THIS Chapter deals with the impact of the Grace of God on the complete make up of man, including the material and immaterial parts, right from creation until regeneration and sanctification. Since Calvinists have written so much about how useless a man is, I took interest to understand the reason for this. This is not to justify man, but to understand who man is. After all, the psalmist writes:

> What is man, that thou art mindful of him? And the son of man that thou visited him? For thou hast made him a little lower than the angels, and hast crowned him with glory and honour. Thou madest him to have dominion over the works of thy hands; thou hast put all things under his feet: Psalm 8: 4-6

ORIGINAL STATE OF MAN

Adam was created in the image and likeness of God. It means that the original man was created in a state of perfect moral values, a perfect mind, and a perfect Will in accord with the Will of God, and a perfect unblemished spirit.

> Lo, this only have I found, that God hath made man upright; but they have sought out many inventions.
> Eccl 7: 29

This state of perfection of man is known as *Adamic* state. The perfect man remained shielded from earthly influences, until...

TRIUNE MAN

It is well accepted that man was created with a material or physical part (body) which houses the immaterial parts (soul and spirit). Before God blew the "breath of life" into Adam's nostrils, he was lifeless.

> And the Lord God formed man of the dust of the ground, and breathed into his nostrils the breath of life; and man became a living soul. Gen. 2: 7

Here, the Spirit of God is what jumpstarted the soul, much like a brand new battery to start a car. God deposited (on loan) part of His Spirit (the breath) in man to sustain his life. When the spirit is low, it needs to be recharged. The spirit is man's active life-force; it represents the spark of light that "quickeneth" (1 Pet. 3:18).

The soul (psyche) is considered the makeup of man; it is what differentiates one man from another. A man can house only one soul. Sometimes the word soul is meant to refer not only to the immaterial part of man but also the material part. Unlike man having a "spirit," man is a soul.

What does the scripture say about body, soul, and spirit? The word "spirit" appears in 236 verses in the Old Testament and in 287 verses in the New Testament. The word "soul" is used in 433 verses in Old Testament and in 55 verses in New Testament. We shall analyze some of them without contradicting the rest.

SPIRIT OF MAN

In the original Greek New Testament, spirit is defined as a *pneuma,* which has to do with air or breath. The word pneumatic, "air pressure", originates from this. The spirit of man operates in a different realm from the soul; it enables man to discern and communicate with the pneumatic or windy movements of other external spirits.

> The wind bloweth where it listeth, and thou hearest the sound thereof, but canst not tell whence it cometh, and whither it goeth: so is every one that is born of the Spirit.
> John 3: 8

Only man's spirit is lodged in the spiritual frame of man. The soul can give residence to other external spirits; the lodged external spirits will be called *extrinsic* spirits while man's spirit will be called *intrinsic* spirit.

> God is a Spirit : and they that worship him must worship him in spirit and in truth. John 4:24

The spirit of man is needed to have relationship with God; it communicates with the Spirit of God and other external spirits in the wind and in the soul.

Intrinsic spirit is given back to God the owner

> Into thine hand I commit my spirit: Ps. 31:5

> Then shall the dust return to the earth as it was: and the spirit shall return unto God who gave it. Eccl. 12: 7

Intrinsic spirit can be quieted but not destroyed

> Then cried he upon me, and spake unto me, saying, Behold, these that go toward the north country have quieted my spirit in the north country. Zech. 6:8

Intrinsic spirit can wear down and be revived

> ...and when he had drunk, his spirit came again, and he revived: Judges 15: 19

God can manipulate intrinsic spirit for His purpose

> The Lord stirred up the spirit of Cyrus king of Persia, that he made a proclamation throughout all his Kingdom, 2Chr. 36:22

> The Lord hath mingled a perverse spirit in the midst thereof: and they have caused Egypt to err in every work thereof, as a drunken man staggereth in his vomit. Isa. 19:14

And the Lord stirred up the spirit of Zerubbabel the son of Shealtiel, governor of Judah, and the spirit of Joshua the son of Josedech, the high priest, and the spirit of all the remnant of the people; and they came and did work in the house of the Lord of hosts, their God, Hag. 1:14

Intrinsic spirit has emotion or inner feeling

And Moses spake so unto the children of Israel: but they hearkened not unto Moses for anguish of spirit, and for cruel bondage. Exo. 6:9

And Hannah answered and said, No, my lord, I am a woman of a sorrowful spirit: 1 Sam. 1:15

Because they provoked his spirit, so that he spake unadvisedly with his lips. Ps. 106:33

As for me, is my complaint to man? and if it were so, why should not my spirit be troubled? Job 21:4

But Jezebel his wife came to him, and said unto him, Why is thy spirit so sad, that thou eatest no bread?
1 Kings 21:5

The sacrifices of God are a broken spirit: a broken and a contrite heart, Ps. 51:17

I remembered God, and was troubled: I complained, and my spirit was overwhelmed. Ps. 77:3

For the Lord hath called thee as a woman forsaken and grieved in spirit, and a wife of youth, when thou wast refused, saith thy God. Isaiah 54:6

And the king said unto them, I have dreamed a dream, and my spirit was troubled to know the dream. Dan. 2:3

I Daniel was grieved in my spirit in the midst of my body, and the visions of my head troubled me. Dan. 7:15

So the spirit lifted me up, and took me away, and I went in bitterness, in the heat of my spirit; but the hand of the Lord was strong upon me. Ezek. 3:14

Intrinsic spirit has Intellect

I call to remembrance my song in the night: I commune with mine own heart: and my spirit made diligent search Ps. 77:6

I have heard the check of my reproach, and the spirit of my understanding causeth me to answer. Job 20:3

Intrinsic spirit as energy

And the meat of his table, and the sitting of his servants, and the attendance of his ministers, and their apparel, and his cupbearers, and his ascent by which he went up unto the house of the Lord; there was no more spirit in her. 1 Kings 10:5

Intrinsic spirit protects the soul

A talebearer revealeth secrets: but he that is of a faithful spirit concealeth the matter. Prov. 11:13

Intrinsic spirit responds to the emotion of the soul

A merry heart maketh a cheerful countenance: but by sorrow of the heart the spirit is broken. Prov. 15:13

Intrinsic spirit has a Will

The spirit indeed is willing, but the flesh is weak. Matt. 26:41

Intrinsic spirit communicates with the Spirit of God

And whose spirit was not steadfast with God (Ps. 78:8)

The spirit of man is the candle of the Lord, searching all the inward parts of the belly. Prov. 20:27

God is a Spirit: and they that worship him must worship him in spirit and in truth. John 4:24

But God hath revealed them unto us by his Spirit: for the Spirit searcheth all things, yea, the deep things of God. 1 Cor. 2:10

But the natural man receiveth not the things of the Spirit of God: for they are foolishness unto him: neither can he know them, because they are spiritually discerned. 1 Cor. 2: 14

Extrinsic spirit can be added to the immaterial part of man

And the spirit entered into me when he spake unto me, and set me upon my feet, that I heard him that spake unto me. Ezek. 2:2

Extrinsic spirits are of two types: clean and unclean. According to the Bible, unclean spirits include any spirit besides the Spirit of God, such as demons and devils.

And when he had called unto him his twelve disciples, he gave them power against unclean spirits, to cast them out, and to heal all manner of sickness and all manner of disease. Matt. 10: 1

Extrinsic Spirit from God is for balance and life

The Spirit of God hath made me, and the breath of the Almighty hath given me life. Job 33:4

Restore unto me the joy of thy salvation; and uphold me with thy free spirit. Ps. 51:12

Extrinsic Spirit from God guides

Then was Jesus led up of the Spirit into the wilderness to be tempted of the devil. Matt. 4: 1

Then the Spirit said unto Philip, Go near, and join thyself to this chariot. Acts 8: 29

Spirit can be removed from man or transferred to man

And the Lord came down in a cloud, and spake unto him, and took of the spirit that was upon him, and gave it unto the seventy elders: Num. 11:25

And Elisha said, I pray thee, let a double portion of thy spirit be upon me. 2 Kings 2:9

Cast me not away from thy presence; and take not thy holy spirit from me. Ps. 51:11

When the even was come, they brought unto him many that were possessed with devils: and he cast out the spirits with his word, and healed all that were sick:
Matt. 8:16

And certain women, which had been healed of evil spirits and infirmities, Mary called Magdalene, out of whom went seven devils, Luke 8: 2

Spirits are indestructible

When the unclean spirit is gone out of a man, he walketh through dry places, seeking rest; and finding none, he saith, I will return unto my house whence I came out. Then goeth he, and taketh to him seven other spirits more wicked than himself; and they enter in, and dwell there: and the last state of that man is worse than the first. Luke 11: 24, 26

Intrinsic spirit can be controlled (responded to by the soul)

He that hath no rule over his own spirit is like a city that is broken down, and without walls. Prov. 25: 28

Man cannot retain or remove spirit from himself

There is no man that hath power over the spirit to retain the spirit; neither hath he power in the day of death: Eccl. 8: 8

Only the Spirit of God can remove extrinsic spirits

But if I cast out devils by the Spirit of God, then the Kingdom of God is come unto you. Matt. 12: 28

Spirit can behave (a state of the heart)

Pride goeth before destruction, and an haughty spirit before a fall. Better it is to be of an humble spirit with the lowly, than to divide the spoil with the proud. Prov. 16: 18-19

The spirit of a man will sustain his infirmity; but a wounded spirit who can bear? Prov. 18: 14

SOUL OF MAN

In order to understand how the soul functions, we have to first examine some biblical references to soul.

Biblical References

The soul is sometimes used like the physical man because the soul transmits decision to the body:

> Or what shall a man give in exchange for his soul? Mark 8:37
>
> Then they that gladly received his word were baptized: and the same day there were added unto them about three thousand souls. Acts 2:41
>
> Then sent Joseph, and called his father Jacob to him, and all his kindred, threescore and fifteen souls. Acts 7:14
>
> Let every soul be subject unto the higher powers. For there is no power but of God: the powers that be are ordained of God. Rom 13:1
>
> Which sometime were disobedient, when once the longsuffering of God waited in the days of Noah, while the ark was a preparing, wherein few, that is, eight souls were saved by water. 1 Pet 3:20
>
> And whatsoever soul it be that doeth any work in that same day, the same soul will I destroy from among his people. Lev. 23:30

Flesh is body and soul combined. In the New Testament, spirit and flesh are used in many instances without referring to the soul.

> But as then he that was born after the flesh persecuted him that was born after the Spirit, even so it is now. Gal. 4:29
>
> For this cause was the Gospel preached also to them that are dead, that they might be judged according to men in the flesh, but live according to God in the spirit. 1 Pet. 4:6
>
> Watch and pray, that ye enter not into temptation: the spirit indeed is willing, but the flesh is weak. Matt. 26:41

That which is born of the flesh is flesh; and that which is born of the Spirit is spirit. John 3: 6

Soul can be lost; unbelievers are often referred to as "lost souls".

For what shall it profit a man, if he shall gain the whole world, and lose his own soul? Mark 8:36

Sin entices the soul

Having eyes full of adultery, and that cannot cease from sin; beguiling unstable souls: an heart they have exercised with covetous practices; cursed children: 2 Pet. 2: 14

God owns souls and recovers only good souls

Behold, all souls are mine; as the soul of the father, so also the soul of the son is mine: the soul that sinneth, it shall die. Ezek. 18: 4

And it shall come to pass, that every soul, which will not hear that prophet, shall be destroyed from among the people. Acts 3: 23

Soul as Emotion transmitted to the body

But if ye will not hear it, my soul shall weep in secrete places for your pride; and my eye will weep sore, and run down with tears... (Jer. 13:17)

For I have satiated the weary soul, and I have replenished every sorrowful soul. Jer. 31: 25

Did I not weep for him that was in trouble? Was not my soul grieved for the poor? (Job 30:25)

And fear came upon every soul: and many wonders and signs were done by the apostles. Acts 2:43

Tribulation and anguish, upon every soul of man that doeth evil, of the Jew first, and also of the Gentile; Rom 2: 9

My soul melteth for heaviness: strengthen thou me according unto thy word. Ps. 119:28

And it came to pass, when she pressed him daily with her words, and urged him, so that his soul was vexed unto death; Judges 16: 16

How long will ye vex my soul, and break me in pieces with words? Job 19:2

Then saith he unto them, My soul is exceeding sorrowful, even unto death: tarry ye here, and watch with me. Matt 26:38

Now is my soul troubled; and what shall I say? Father, save me from this hour: but for this cause came I unto this hour. John 12:27

And the fruits that thy soul lusted after are departed from thee, and all things which were dainty and goodly are departed from thee, and thou shalt find them no more at all. Rev. 18:14

Soul as Intellect

When wisdom entereth into thine heart, and knowledge is pleasant unto thy soul; Prov. 2:10

I will praise thee; for I am fearfully and wonderfully made: marvellous are thy works; and that my soul knoweth right well. Ps. 139:14

Soul as Heart

But if from thence thou shalt seek the Lord thy God, thou shalt find him, if thou seek him with all thy heart and with all thy soul. Deut. 4:29

And the multitude of them that believed were of one heart and of one soul: Acts 4:32

Soul as Mind

Forasmuch as we have heard, that certain which went out from us have troubled you with words, subverting your souls, saying, Ye must be circumcised, and keep the law: to whom we gave no such commandment:
Acts 15: 24

(Yea, a sword shall pierce through thy own soul also,) that the thoughts of many hearts may be revealed.
Luke 2: 35

All the believers were one in heart and mind (NIV). All the multitude of them that believed were of one heart and of one soul (KJV). (Acts 4:32)

Soul as Will

The soul of the wicked desireth evil: his neighbour findeth no favour in his eyes. Prov. 21:10

Soul as Will, Power, or Heart

And thou shalt love the Lord thy God with all thine heart, and with all thy soul, and with all thy might.
Deut. 6: 5

Thou shalt love the Lord thy God with all thy heart and with all thy soul with all thy strength and with all thy mind.... (Matt. 22: 37, Luke 10:27)

The word "might" or "strength" here means latent power or Will of man.

The Five Faculties

From all the biblical references, we can infer that the soul (psyche) is the human engine that houses a combination of five faculties: *Heart*, *Intellect*, *Mind*, *Will*, and *Emotion.* These five faculties (I call them "the five fingers of soul") define the man and each is unique to each man. Experiments, which include research (Intellect), exploration (Mind), execution (Heart), test (Emotion), and conclusion (Will), are carried out in the soul. In the scripture, soul is sometimes referred to as the "Heart" because it is there man's core Values or Virtues, such as goodness, kindness, honesty, and so on, are kept. A soft heart interprets as kindness and a hardened heart is wickedness or stubbornness. The fall of man usually stems from the Heart and Emotion which are the two faculties that have options for decision making; this will further be explained under "Illustration of Man". The Mind keeps man's thoughts and conscience, and the Intellect keeps knowledge and wisdom. Emotion (man's inner feelings) is the weakest faculty of the soul while Will is the strongest. Will is the part of the soul that makes the final decisions that are transmitted to the body. Will interacts with the other faculties: mind, intellect, heart, and emotion. Will is the strength of man, the latent power so to speak. We shall cover the Will of man in more detail in the next section.

As we shall see later on, after regeneration, God also dwells in man's soul (heart) to protect it from satanic assaults and to communicate with the intrinsic spirit. Man's soul is open to attack and deception of the enemy because quite often the Will succumbs to responses from emotions, the weakest faculty, to take decisions. God then had to institute the universal grace to protect life of soul, urge Will, increase wisdom and knowledge of Him, and guide emotions. The soul performs rational and intellectual functions to actively work and make choices. But, *the rational will never capture the wind (spirit)!* This is why man is unable to discern or choose God with his soul alone.

BODY OF MAN

Body is the physical part of man. The body responds to the soul. The body communicates with the soul through its five senses: touch, smell, hear, see, and taste; the soul transmits back its decision to the body through these senses.

Idols do not have senses

> And there ye shall serve gods, the work of men's hands, wood and stone, which neither see, nor hear, nor eat, nor smell. Deut. 4: 28

Taste and soul

> For the vile person will speak villany, and his heart will work iniquity, to practise hypocrisy, and to utter error against the Lord, to make empty the soul of the hungry, and he will cause the drink of the thirsty to fail. Is. 32: 6

All her people sigh, they seek bread; they have given their pleasant things for meat to relieve the soul: see, O Lord, and consider; for I am become vile. Lam. 1: 11

Touch and soul

Or if a soul touch any unclean thing, whether it be a carcase of an unclean beast... Lev. 5: 2

The things that my soul refused to touch are as my sorrowful meat. Job 6: 7

Sight and soul

Have mercy upon me, O Lord, for I am in trouble: mine eye is consumed with grief, yea, my soul and my belly. Ps. 31: 9

The soul of the wicked desireth evil: his neighbour findeth no favour in his eyes. Prov. 21: 10

For these things I weep; mine eye, mine eye runneth down with water, because the comforter that should relieve my soul is far from me: my children are desolate, because the enemy prevailed. Lam. 1: 16

Behold, I will profane my sanctuary, the excellency of your strength, the desire of your eyes, and that which your soul pitieth; and your sons and your daughters whom ye have left shall fall by the sword. Ezek. 24: 21

Having eyes full of adultery, and that cannot cease from sin; beguiling unstable souls: an heart they have exercised with covetous practices; cursed children: 2 Pet. 2: 14

He shall see of the travail of his soul, and shall be satisfied: by his knowledge shall my righteous servant justify many; for he shall bear their iniquities. Isa. 53: 11

He shall redeem their soul from deceit and violence: and precious shall their blood be in his sight Ps. 72: 14

Hearing and soul

And if a soul sin, and hear the voice of swearing, and is a witness, whether he hath seen or known of it; if he do not utter it, then he shall bear his iniquity. Lev. 5: 1

Whoso is partner with a thief hateth his own soul: he heareth cursing, and bewrayeth it not. Prov. 29:24

My soul longeth, yea, even fainteth for the courts of the Lord: my heart and my flesh crieth out for the living God. Ps. 84: 2

I cannot hold my peace, because thou hast heard, O my soul, the sound of the trumpet, the alarm of war.
Jer. 4:19

And it shall come to pass, that every soul, which will not hear that prophet, shall be destroyed from among the people. Acts 3: 23

Smell and soul

Ointment and perfume rejoice the heart: so doth the sweetness of a man's friend by hearty counsel.
Prov. 27: 9

For in that she hath poured this ointment on my body, she did it for my burial. Matt. 26: 12

Body can resist soul's decision

Dearly beloved, I beseech you as strangers and pilgrims, abstain from fleshly lusts, which war against the soul;
1 Pet. 2: 11

Both body and soul need spirit for life

> For as the body without the spirit is dead, so faith without works is dead also. James 2: 26

COMPARISON OF SOUL AND SPIRIT

General Characteristics

Although Christians generally believe that man has two distinct parts: the material and immaterial parts, however, there is confusion as to whether the immaterial part is one or two, that is, whether soul and spirit are one and the same or not. The belief that our immaterial part consists of two parts is called *trichotomy*. It teaches that humans are composed of body, soul, and spirit. On the other hand, the belief that soul and spirit are interchangeable terms for one immaterial self is known as *dichotomy*.

As we have seen, both soul and spirit have close characteristics in terms of faculties. They both have emotion and intellect. Also, as we shall see later, emotion and heart are related while intellect and mind are also related. So, both soul and spirit appears to be the same to justify dichotomy. The Greek and Hebrew translations are also similar in the line of "breath" or "life" for both soul and spirit. But Hebrews 4:12 seems to indicate that there is a difference:

> For the word of God is quick, and powerful, and sharper than any twoedged sword, piercing even to the dividing asunder of soul and spirit, and of the joints and marrow, and is a discerner of the thoughts and intents of the heart. (Heb 4:12)

If both soul and spirit are life givers, what then is the distinction if there is? There are two basic distinctions being offered by trichotomists and three others (3 to 5 below) are inferred from studies in this book:

1. The soul is considered as the bridge between the spiritual realm and the physical realm (body), between our godly self and our earthly self. This implies that the soul communicates between the body and spirit.
2. In terms of relationships, the soul is man's need for horizontal relationship with other men while the spirit is man's need for vertical relationship with God.
3. The soul always stays with man until death. However, the spirit may dislodge from man when he is in a state of unconsciousness and re-lodge when he is conscious; this may explain dreams, witchcraft, and other "cosmic" phenomena.
4. In this study, as seen above, a soul may end up in hell or in Heaven while the spirit always returns to God.
5. Also, in this study, it seems intrinsic spirit may be renewed completely while soul can only be "refurbished".

Biblical Characteristics

Let us explore other biblical distinctions between soul and spirit.

Man has only one soul, but he can house multiple spirits

> But my servant Caleb, because he had another spirit with him, and hath followed me fully... Numb 14:24

Sin and death are always only associated with the soul and not the spirit

To deliver their soul from death, and to keep them alive in famine. Ps 33:19

They rewarded me evil for good to the spoiling of my soul. Ps. 35:12

Then said I, Ah Lord God! behold, my soul hath not been polluted: for from my youth up even till now have I not eaten of that which dieth of itself, or is torn in pieces; neither came there abominable flesh into my mouth. Eze 4:14

Her princes in the midst thereof are like wolves ravening the prey, to shed blood, and to destroy souls, to get dishonest gain. Eze 22:27

When my soul fainted within me I remembered the Lord: and my prayer came in unto thee, into thine holy temple. Jonah 2:7

Will the Lord be pleased with thousands of rams, or with ten thousands of rivers of oil? shall I give my firstborn for my transgression, the fruit of my body for the sin of my soul? Micah 6:7

Thou hast consulted shame to thy house by cutting off many people, and hast sinned against thy soul. Hab 2: 10

Say, I pray thee, thou art my sister: that it may be well with me for thy sake; and my soul shall live because of thee. Gen. 12: 13

And when he had opened the fifth seal, I saw under the altar the souls of them that were slain for the word of God, and for the testimony which they held: Rev. 6: 9

And the second angel poured out his vial upon the sea; and it became as the blood of a dead man: and every living soul died in the sea. Rev. 16: 3

Because thou wilt not leave my soul in hell, neither wilt thou suffer thine Holy One to see corruption. Acts 2: 27

Let him know, that he which converteth the sinner from the error of his way shall save a soul from death, and shall hide a multitude of sins. James 5: 20

But the spirit can fail

For I will not contend for ever, neither will I be always wroth: for the spirit should fail before me, and the souls which I have made. Isaiah 57: 16

Spirit seeks God and soul makes decision

With my soul have I desired thee in the night; yea, with my spirit within me will I seek thee early: for when thy judgments are in the earth, the inhabitants of the world will learn righteousness. Isa 26: 9

Spirit guides the soul

Seeing ye have purified your souls in obeying the truth through the Spirit unto unfeigned love of the brethren, see that ye love one another with a pure heart fervently: 1 Pet 1: 22

Evil can only attack the soul not the spirit

Sing unto the Lord, praise ye the Lord: for he hath delivered the soul of the poor from the hand of evildoers. Jer. 20: 13

For the enemy hath persecuted my soul; Ps. 143: 3

The soul can be destroyed in hell

And fear not them which kill the body, but are not able to kill the soul: but rather fear him which is able to destroy both soul and body in hell. Matt. 10: 28

He seeing this before spake of the resurrection of Christ, that His soul was not left in hell, neither his flesh did see corruption Acts 2:31

External spirit can be added to intrinsic spirit but no other soul can be added to soul

And I have filled him with the spirit of God, Exo. 31: 3

Regard not them that have familiar spirits, Lev. 19: 31

Soul chooses external spirit to house

And the soul that turneth after such as have familiar spirits, and after wizards, to go a whoring after them, I will even set my face against that soul, and will cut him off from among his people. Lev. 20: 6

Soul needs salvation not spirit

For the redemption of their soul is precious, Ps. 49: 8
Truly my soul waiteth upon God: from him cometh my salvation. Ps. 62: 1

For what shall it profit a man, if he shall gain the whole world, and lose his own soul? Mark 8: 36

Wherefore lay apart all filthiness and superfluity of naughtiness, and receive with meekness the engrafted word, which is able to save your souls. James 1: 21

Receiving the end of your faith, even the salvation of your souls. 1 Pet 1: 9

Both intrinsic spirit and soul can be renewed. This is very important because it explains the purpose of salvation.

> And I will give them one heart, and I will put a new spirit within you; and I will take the stony heart out of their flesh, and will give them an heart of flesh: Ezekiel 11: 19
>
> Create in me a clean heart, O God; and renew a right spirit within me. Ps. 51:10
>
> Cast away from you all your transgressions, whereby ye have transgressed; and make you a new heart and a new spirit: for why will ye die, O house of Israel? Eze. 18: 31

WILL OF MAN

We dealt at length on the state of man because it is important in the understanding of Will. Will is a latent power made available to man in creation to enable him to take initiatives and to make good choices. It is the decision making faculty of man's soul. Synonyms of Will are: *choice, decision, psyche, awareness*. Before there can be any choice, options must be made available to the Will by other faculties. The options come from the Heart and Emotion faculties (explained further under "Illustration" and "regeneration"). God has His Will for man and gave each man a Will to enable him to make right choices (well, that was the original intent).

PROOF OF WILL

> And the Lord God commanded the man, saying of every tree of the garden thou mayest freely eat: but of the tree of the knowledge of good and evil, thou shalt not eat of it: for in the day that thou eatest thereof thou shalt surely die. (Gen. 2:16-17)

Application Study Bible commentary:

> Rather than physically preventing him from eating, God gave Adam a choice and, thus the possibility of choosing wrongly. Why would God place a tree in the garden and then forbid Adam to eat from it? God wanted Adam to obey, but He gave him the freedom to choose. Without choice, Adam would have been, like a prisoner, forced to obey.

Will is the first potential available to mankind before sin entered the world; as it will be explained later, it can no longer function on its own without the universal grace. Will is part of God's architecture of man; it was factored in the creation of man, and could have been because of satan's fall.

PURPOSE OF WILL

Will is given to man to respond to God's Will. Will was the latent power given to Adam to help keep him in the Garden of Eden (Paradise) for ever, but sin corrupted it. There were two reasons Adam received a Will:

1. To assist him to choose to obey God (see Chapter 7);

2. To assist him in managing his responsibilities by making good choices (see Chapter 3):

> And God blessed them, and God said unto them, be fruitful, and multiply, and replenish the earth, and subdue it: and have dominion over the fish of the sea, and over the fowl of the air, and over every living thing that moveth upon the earth (Gen. 1:28)

Without a Will, Adam would have been like a robot not able to make any decision of his own; the body would be responding straight away to Emotion and Heart. If we examine the two purposes of Will given to Adam as stated above, one was to help him maintain a good relationship with God, and the other was to help him manage his resources. We can recall that later in life, God gave Moses the Ten Commandments in two slabs of stone; to love God and to love our neighbour. Also, these two purposes are what is required to reach the Kingdom of God: salvation and good works. God has always wanted these two things from man: a good relationship with Him and a good relationship with his environment.

CONSCIENCE AND WILL

God created man in a perfect state until his Will got corrupted. Adam's fall corrupted the Will of man. To help man make good choices, God endowed man with universal gifts that work with his Will. Universal grace assists to fix the corrupted Will. Without it, man is incapable of making any good choices on his own and can not function in line with God's Will because of the corrupted nature of his Will; in short, human Will is useless without universal grace. Universal grace manifests in several forms; one is for life preservation that no man can resist or not respond to; and there are others that he may not respond to and cause him to make wrong choices. Some of the universal gifts that assist the Will are conscience and repentance.

LIMITATION OF WILL

Will of man (now guided by universal grace) has limited ability. It still does not give man the ability to choose to save himself from fall because when it was given to Adam there was no need for any salvation. Man inherited the guilt of sin from Adam and therefore Will does not enable man to choose to save himself. However, universal grace can only work with the Holy Spirit to "urge" Will but it is not sufficient to work Will to effectuate connection to God, and this is where the *special grace* comes in. Man still has to rely on the special grace of God for salvation, even after making the right choice to obey him:

> For He saith unto Moses, I will have mercy on whom I will have mercy, and I will have compassion on whom I will have compassion. (Rom. 9:14)

This mercy of God comes in the form of special grace after Jesus paid the price. Man now relies on Jesus for salvation.

CONSEQUENCE OF CHOICE

Blessing goes with obedience to God's Will and cursing goes with disobedience to His Will.

> I have set before you life and death, blessing and cursing: therefore choose life, that both thou and thy seed may live (Deut. 30:19)

VIEWS ON WILL

The quotations below are retrieved from www.ccel.org, www.newadvent.org, and www.freewill-predestination.com.

> It is understood that in order for Man to have true free choice, he must not only have inner free will, but also an environment in which a choice between obedience and disobedience exists. God thus created the world such that both good and evil can operate freely. (David Bennett)

Ignatius of Antioch (martyred 97-110 AD):

> If any one is truly religious, he is a man of God; but if he is irreligious, he is a man of the devil, made such, not by nature, but by his own choice.

Clement of Alexandria (martyred 190 AD)

> Neither praise nor condemnation, neither rewards nor punishments, are right if the soul does not have the power of choice and avoidance, if evil is involuntary.

> God works together with willing souls. But if the person abandons his eagerness, the spirit from God is also restrained. To save the unwilling is the act of one using

> compulsion; but to save the willing, that of one showing grace

In the last quotation, "God works together with willing souls" means responding to universal grace. Also, it is not the spirit of God that is restrained, but it is the man not responding to the universal grace and causing him to make wrong choices. No, God does not force man to make the right choice.

Irenaeus (written about 180 AD, martyred 202 AD):

> Chap XXXVII: Men are possessed of Free Will, and endowed with the faculty of making a choice. It is not true, therefore, that some are by nature good, and others bad.
>
> Chap XXXIX: Man is endowed with the faculty of distinguishing good and evil; so that, without compulsion, he has the power, by his own Will and choice, to perform God's Commandments, by doing which he avoids the evils prepared for the rebellious.

Justin Martyr (martyred 162-168 AD):

> Man acts by his own free will and not by fate.
>
> Unless humans have the power of avoiding evil and choosing good by free choice, they are not accountable for their actions-whatever they may be.... For neither would a man be worthy of reward or praise if he did not of himself choose the good, but was merely created for that end. Likewise, if a man were evil, he would not deserve punishment, since he was not evil of himself, being unable to do anything else than what he was made for.

ORIGIN OF WILL

If God had created man without a Will, he would not be able to make wrong choices. When I sought the Lord to understand what caused Him to let man have a Will, the Holy Spirit directed me to study the book of Job; and I did. The analysis that follows is my own interpretation of the origin of Will from the story of Job. Scholars have suggested that Job's event took place during the time of the patriarchs. Here is how it all began:

> Now there was a day when the sons of God came to present themselves before the Lord, and satan also came. And the Lord said unto satan, Whence comest thou? Then satan answered the Lord, and said, From going to and fro in the earth, and from walking up and down in it. And the Lord said unto satan, Hast thou considered my servant Job, that there is none like him in the earth, a perfect and an upright man, one that feareth God, and escheweth evil? Job 1:6-8; 2:1-3

First of all, we notice that satan is always walking up and down on earth. Secondly, the fact that the above conversations between God and satan occurred twice in the book of Job suggests that there was an ongoing "cosmic conflict" between God and satan over obedience of man (or simply, a battle for man's soul) ever since satan was deported from Heaven and causing Adam to fall. Remember that the soul can either end up in hell or in Heaven. In the above conversation, it was God who initiated the challenge (perhaps God didn't mean it as a challenge but satan was opportunistic); it appears that in a previous challenge, satan scored a point and God wanted to prove a case. God wanted to show satan that He has servants on earth who obey Him and He is in control of His Will. But satan also wanted to prove that those who obey God do so because He makes them to be comfortable.

> Then satan answered the Lord, and said, Doth Job fear God for nought? Hast thou made an hedge about him, and about his house, and about all that he hath on every side? Job 1:9

But, God eventually won this contest. Here is what I postulate: when Adam was being created, satan dared God that man would not obey Him and would rather follow satan's counsel. In order to test this challenge, God gave man Will to enable him to be able to choose good from evil, but satan eventually scored his point and made man's Will to be corrupted. Since then, winning man's living soul becomes a battle between God and satan. This is discussed below in detail under "Regeneration" which is under "Illustration of Man".

There are several other things to learn from the book of Job:

1. God did not answer Job's questions but instead asked him 85 questions (Job 38-41) all relating to His Sovereignty; not that He wanted Job to answer them, but to let Job know some of the ordinances in Heaven and that we must submit to His power and sovereignty;
2. God is just;
3. God made Job to pray for his friends who blasphemed before He could bless him anew (Job 42:10); this is again God's two purposes of creation of man at work; Job con-

nected to God and then helped others before he received his blessings;
4. God is not evil, but allows good and evil to coexist;
5. Man's knowledge and wisdom are inferior to God's and man can never totally understand Him.

FALL OF MAN

ORIGINAL SIN

God created the Heaven and earth and everything on earth. After creation, God was pleased: "And God saw everything He had made, and behold, it was very good" (Gen. 1:31). God does not sin:

> Therefore hearken unto me, ye men of understanding: far be it from God, that He should do wickedness; and from the Almighty, that He should commit iniquity.
> Job 34:10

So, who created sin?

> He that committeth sin is of the devil; for the devil sinneth from the beginning. I John 3: 8

The devil was the first creature to sin, so he created sin. And how did sin enter the man's world? Adam disobeyed God and transmitted sin from satan to the earth.

> Wherefore, as by one man sin entered into the world, and death by sin; and so death passed upon all men, for all have sinned. (Rom 5:12)

Since Adam's sin, each human inherits the guilt of sin from the parents, and it all started with Adam.

> Who can say, I have made my heart clean, I am pure from my sin? Prov. 20: 9

> For there is not a just man upon earth, that doeth good, and sinneth not. Eccl. 7: 20

God did not cause Adam to disobey Him; otherwise man wouldn't have been created in God's image. The Bible tells us that God hates sin and that sin can't enter Heaven.

TRANSMISSION OF GUILT OF SIN

Man inherits the guilt of sin right from Adam and it is transmitted to men at birth. Sin is like a gene. The original sin has created dark spots in man's soul.

> Behold, I was shapen in iniquity; and in sin did my mother conceive me. Ps. 51: 5

The reason why man inherits the guilt of sin will be explained under "Illustration of Man" below.

ORIGIN OF EVIL

Evil had already occurred before Adam sinned, either in the garden or at the time of satan's fall. Adam knew or did no evil before the tree of knowledge was planted.

> ... the tree of life also in the midst of the garden, and the tree of knowledge of good and evil. (Gen. 2:9)

Calvinist Predestinarian Arthur Pink in "*the total depravity of man*" wrote:

> Sin was the original evil. Before it entered the universe there was no evil:

His statement here is right, but his assertion that man brought evil to the earth cannot be true because the tree of knowledge of good and evil was planted before Adam; so, evil was done before Adam.

DEPRAVITY OF MAN

Ever since sin came to the earth, man has not been able to not to sin. The soul of the natural man has been corrupted and cannot function properly. Only God can talk to man. Man can only communicate back to God through regeneration. When the Bible says:

> For the wages of sin is death; (Rom 6: 23)

What died is the soul. Communication between the spirit of the natural man and the Spirit of God is broken.

> The LORD looked down from Heaven upon the children of men, to see if there were any that did understand, and seek God. They are all gone aside, they are all together become filthy: there is none that doeth good, no, not one. Ps. 14: 2-3; 53:2-3 (Rom 3:11-12)

> For all have sinned, and come short of the glory of God;
> Rom 3: 23

The study in this book agrees with some established doctrines on Depravity of Man, right from Augustine's debate with Pelagius. This book makes the following statement:

> The soul of man is inherently corrupted by sin in every aspect of his being. Because of this, the natural man lacks the ability to choose God, and Adam and his descendants are not able not to sin. Man still has the freedom of the will to make his choices. However, his choices are all determined by his corrupt nature, and in himself he has no ability to choose God to save himself.

All existing major doctrines, of Augustine, Calvin, Arminius, and Wesley, also affirm depravity. It is a common agreement. However, there is an exception with the Calvinists assertion from Arthur Pink's statement below:

> Here, then, are the ramifications of human depravity. The fall has blinded man s mind, hardened his heart, disordered his affections, corrupted his conscience, disabled his will, so that there is "no soundness" in him (Isa. 1:6), "no good thing" in him (Rom. 7:18). (Arthur Pink)

Pink's statements are accepted except for the disabling of the Will part; it is exaggerated. Man's Will is not disabled but corrupted just as he puts it for other faculties. That is the more reason the word "total" is avoided (as in Total Depravity) in this book.

ILLUSTRATION OF MAN

The diagrammatical illustration of man from Adamic state to unregenerate state, and up to a sanctified state, are received through the guidance of the Holy Spirit. I believe the Holy Spirit has purposely revealed this, perhaps for scientific and social benefits. In this section, we will use our studies in the three previous sections: "Original State of Man", "Triune Man", "Will of Man", and "Fall of Man" to understand the importance of grace on the working of the body, soul, and spirit of man. This will be done through illustrations.

THE SOUL

Under the "Triune Man" section above, it was shown that the soul of man has five faculties; they will generally be referred to as the "Five Fingers of Soul". The five faculties are *Heart*, *Intellect*, *Mind*, *Will*, and *Emotion*. Each of these faculties of the soul has elements which could run into billions. Samples of elements are given in Table 4.1. For every *good element* God creates, satan has his own counterfeit element, to be called *evil element*. Sin introduced the evil elements into the soul. The last two columns of Table 4.1 on satan's attack will be discussed later.

Table 4.1: The Five Fingers of Soul (HIM-WE)

Faculty	Sample Elements	Satan's Attack Method	
		regenerate	unregenerate
Heart	Kindness, Humility, Pride, Honesty, Generosity, Humanity, Integrity, Wickedness, Meek, Adultery, Life	Hardening, Guilt	Deception, Hardening
Intellect	Knowledge, Wisdom, Intelligence, Talent, Memory, Imagination	Trickery, Counterfeit, Delay	Trickery, Fraud
Mind	Thought, Conscience, Perception	Diversion	Manipulation
Will	Strength, Decision	Persuasion	Urging
Emotion	Anger, Fear, Anguish, Temper, Joy, Happiness, Hunger, Agony, Lust, Envy, Excitement, Sorrow, Shame, Remorse, Compassion, Empathy, Love, Hatred	Temptation, Guilt	Luring, Baiting, Enticing

Heart and Emotion are closely related. Only in the Heart and Emotion are switches; that is, two options are always available for the elements, either between good or evil, yes or no, do or don't, that can be actively transmitted to the body in expression of a behavior. Examples of switches are:

> Acceptance–Rejection; Anger–Calm; Anxiety–Ease; Boredom–Excitement; Boldness–Shyness; Compassion–Coldness; Despair–Hope; Pride–Humility; Optimism–Pessimism; Joy–Sadness; Love–Hatred; Shame–Pleasure; Surprise–Anticipation; Trust–Distrust; War-Peace

The relationship between Heart and Emotion definitely needs further study; however, it seems that it is a *cause-effect* relationship; the cause is in Emotion and the effect (action) is in the Heart; the following passage demonstrates this:

> But I say unto you, That whosoever looketh on a woman to lust after her hath committed adultery with her already in his heart. Matt 5: 28

Lust (the cause) is emotional and adultery (the effect) is in the Heart. Intellect and Mind are also closely related; some elements such as imagination can be Intellect (as in creativity) or Mind (as in thought).

THE INTRINSIC SPIRIT

The intrinsic spirit is the spirit of man and it resides in the spiritual frame. It is the source of energy for man, his battery so to speak. It gives life to the Heart faculty of the soul. Sometimes the spirit can be low. We will explain how it can be recharged later.

Security

The spirit communicates with the Heart faculty where the life element resides. Satan cannot attack the spiritual frame; only the Holy Spirit has direct access to the frame and can monitor the activities there. That frame is secure and protected. Satan can only take man's life through the Heart (where the life element is) if the Will allows him entrance into the soul. For the unregenerate man, the intrinsic spirit has no ability to communicate with God (shown in Figure

4.2), but God can manipulate it as seen previously from the scripture.

> The Lord stirred up the spirit of Cyrus king of Persia, that he made a proclamation throughout all his Kingdom, 2 Chr. 36: 22

Quantization

Spirits in general can be viewed as *living* air particles, that is, like *living* photons (light particles). Photons are quanta, that is, packets of energy at different energy levels (physicists know what this means). Quantization means that the magnitude of energy can take on only certain discrete values, rather than any value. Earlier, it was mentioned that extrinsic spirit can be removed or transferred, and only God can do that.

> And the Lord came down in a cloud, and spake unto him, and took of the spirit that was upon him, and gave it unto the seventy elders: Num. 11:25

> And Elisha said, I pray thee, let a double portion of thy spirit be upon me. 2 Kings 2:9

Although the spirits being transferred in the above two passages were interpreted to be extrinsic; however, in the first passage, it could also be intrinsic. Extrinsic spirits from God are either *spiritual special gifts* or *spiritual universal gifts*; the spiritual universal gifts reside permanently in the soul while the spiritual special gifts are obtained after regeneration and they reside in the spiritual frame. The universal gifts, discussed in Chapter 3, will also be discussed further under regeneration below. In the two verses above, the spirits mentioned are definitely not spiritual universal gifts.

In the first passage, God took of the spirit (note the singularity) of Moses and distributed it over seventy elders to energize them. Obviously Moses' energy level in this case was reduced. In the case of Elisha (the second passage), the spirit cannot be intrinsic because it has to return to God when one departs (also seen previously); Elisha was asking for a double portion, he cannot get a double portion of the intrinsic spirit. In the case below, the spirits are unclean, so they were removed from the soul. Unclean spirits cannot be housed in the spiritual frame of man.

> When the even was come, they brought unto him many that were possessed with devils: and he cast out the spirits with his word, Matt. 8: 16

State of Unconsciousness

One other point mentioned earlier is that, a spirit also has the five faculties that the soul has, so the spirit is a complete being. That is why many people confuse it with the soul. When a quantum of spirit departs from the man, it departs as a complete being with a certain amount of energy. We can now have a better understanding of the concept of consciousness and unconsciousness. When a man is in a state of unconsciousness, such as sleeping or meditating, a quantum of his intrinsic spirit (or the entire spirit) might depart from his body. When someone is sleeping, the Heart serves as the reservoir for life. The intrinsic spirit is perhaps in a spiritual "cosmos" as it is reflected in dreams. If the spirit departs completely and the reservoir is exhausted before the spirit returns, the soul dies and goes to either Heaven or hell. A friend of mine just lost his son, a devoted Christian, always in the presence of the Lord. He was healthy the night before he slept and woke up no more the following morning. Autopsies performed in two different laboratories revealed nothing was the cause of death. His spirit went to the Lord and the Lord retained him. This is not intended to scare anyone, but to demonstrate that anytime you wake up in the morning, you should be giving thanks to God for keeping you alive. He owns the spirit; He can reclaim it when you are in a state of unconsciousness, like sleeping.

ADAMIC STATE

Adam had a perfect intrinsic spirit and a perfect soul without blemish (that is, no evil elements). Each of the faculties in the soul was perfect and uncorrupted. Adam sinned and the soul became corrupted with all the faculties affected. The Will is the Head of all the faculties. It is there the final decisions are taken. Satan must have attacked the Intellect faculty of Eve. She was tricked. I believe satan usually attacks the Intellect and Emotion faculties of a woman and the Will faculty of a man to break a marriage.

> And the serpent said unto the woman, Ye shall not surely die; for God doth know that in the day ye eat thereof, then your eyes shall be opened, and ye shall be as gods, knowing good and evil. Gen. 3: 4-6

Adam had a perfect clean soul

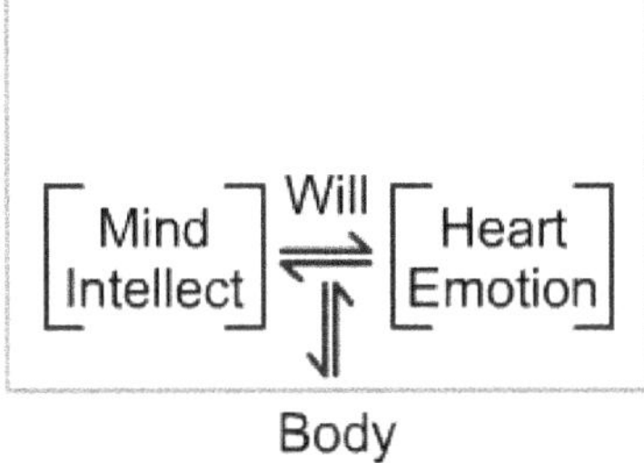

Then satan attacked

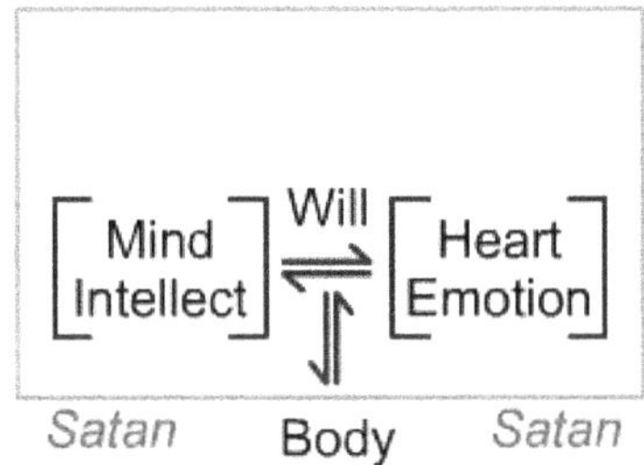

Adam sinned, the soul is corrupted

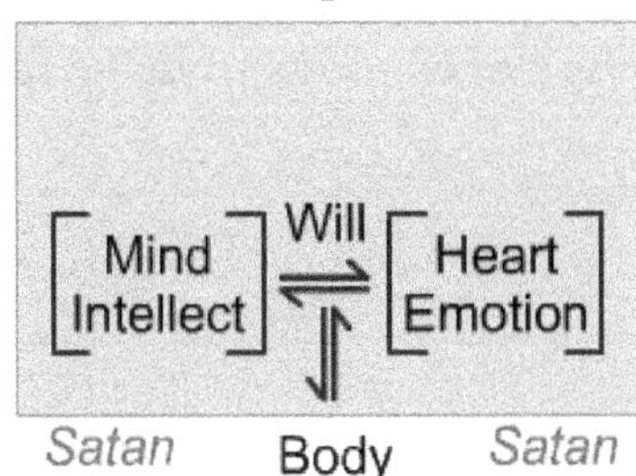

Figure 4.1: Adamic State of Soul

The spiritual realm for Adam is not illustrated in Figure 4.1. Satan does not have access to the spiritual realm of man; otherwise, he would not let man to exist. Therefore, the spirit can not be corrupted. In Figure 4.1, the soul is darkened after corruption.

What is the corruption of the soul?

The options that are created in the Heart and Emotion as discussed above are the result of the *evil elements* that sin introduced into the soul. Sin brought in counterfeit duplicates of God's perfect elements. God warned Adam against this:

> But of the tree of the knowledge of good and evil, thou shalt not eat of it: for in the day that thou eatest thereof thou shalt surely die. Gen. 2: 17

We see that the death here is the evil elements that entered into the soul to counteract the good elements.

Why does man inherit the guilt of Adam's sin?

Since God did not recreate man, the evil elements permanently form part of the network of the soul. It becomes like a gene. It is transmitted to man at birth. It is only sanctification that can remove the evil elements from the soul.

Why is Jesus without sin?

> And ye know that he was manifested to take away our sins; and in him is no sin. I John 3: 5

If Jesus had been conceived through the sexual union of a man and woman, He would have also inherited the guilt of sin common to all humans. Jesus was born of a virgin without any human involvement. Jesus is the only person who lived as a human without transmitted sin.

UNREGENERATE STATE

For those unfamiliar with the term, unregenerate means someone who has not received salvation; that is, the natural man. After Adam's sin, the soul of man was filled with so many evil elements that he was depraved. It was always one evil after another. Only Noah was found perfect during his generation. The natural man cannot communicate with God; the intrinsic spirit is not connected to God.

> But the natural man receiveth not the things of the Spirit of God: for they are foolishness unto him: neither can he know them, because they are spiritually discerned.
> 1 Cor. 2: 14

Spiritual Universal Gifts

After the flood, God granted man universal gifts through His universal grace, to augment the good elements. Adam also had universal gifts (the good elements); however, universal grace introduced new elements, such as *conscience*, to assist the soul in making decisions, and *remorse* that leads to repentance, hence salvation. The new universal gifts could number in the millions. It is difficult to ascertain which characteristic elements of man are in the original Adamic state and which are from the universal grace. According to Hanko, the Arminians recognize this kind of universal grace:

> The Arminians taught a "common grace," that is a grace of God common to all. The Arminians meant by common grace those gifts which man did not lose when he fell. (Hanko, April 6, 2009)

Universal gifts are given to all the faculties of the soul.

> For God hath not given us the spirit of fear; but of power, and of love, and of a sound mind. 2 Tim. 1: 7

The following are suggested examples of universal gifts for the Heart and Emotion faculties:

> Affection, Apathy, Awe, Calmness, Compassion, Contentment, Dedication, Desire, Ecstasy, Empathy, Enthusiasm, Gratification, Gratitude, Happiness, Hope, Inspiration, Interest,·Kindness,·Love, Passion, Patience, Pity, Purposeful, Regret, Remorse, Repentance, Sympathy

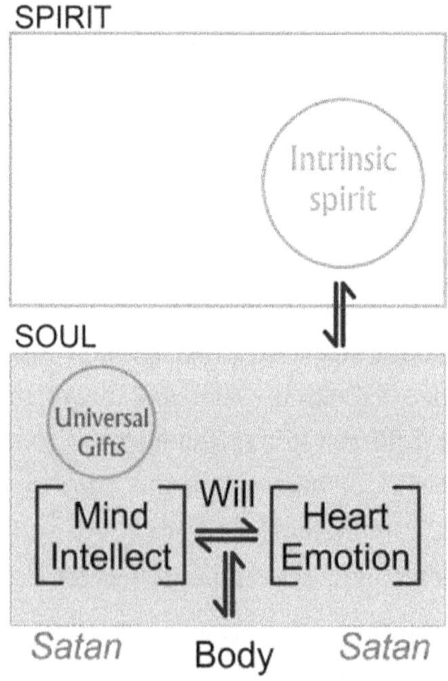

Figure 4.2: Triune State of Unregenerate Man

Figure 4.2 illustrates the triune state (Body, Soul, and Spirit) of the unregenerate man. Spiritual universal gifts are gifts from universal grace and they reside in the soul. This has been discussed in Chapter 3.

The working mechanism in the soul is complex, but the Will takes the final decision and passes it through some (unknown) mechanism to the body for execution. Here are some related quotes (on mechanisms of characteristic elements) selected from Mike Murdock's 365 wisdom keys:

> Every problem is always a wisdom problem.
>
> When your heart decides the destination, your mind will design the map to reach it.
>
> Your focus decides your feelings.
>
> The true function of wisdom is order.
>
> Loneliness is not the absence of affection, but the absence of direction.
>
> Patience is the weapon that forces deception to reveal itself.
>
> A tired mind rarely makes good decisions.
>
> Creativity is the search for options; focus is the elimination of them.

There are billions of possibilities of such mechanisms and permutations.

Science and Soul

Some of the elements (good and evil) in each faculty of the soul are given in Table 4.1. There could be billions of elements. The network of soul to the five senses of the body looks to me like the nervous system of man. Out of curiosity, I researched developments in neurology. It is amazing what I discovered. Here are some facts:

1. Science is still unable to understand the working of the human brain; this shows God's supremacy over all things. Man can never by his wisdom uncover God.

   > Then I beheld all the work of God, that a man cannot find out the work that is done under the sun: because though a man labour to seek it out, yet he shall not find it; yea further; though a wise man think to know it, yet shall he not be able to find it. Eccl 8: 17

2. The brain has billions of neurons; in our analogy here, these neurons are the elements of the five faculties of the soul. Yes! The problem brain scientists are facing is the network of neurons which seems to be well coordinated, but they are just too numerous for scientists to figure out. God is the best network engineer ever. So, with our analogy, each man has billions of characteristic elements (spiritual universal gifts). That is why no two souls can have the same exact personalities with all the possible permutations. God is the greatest mathematician ever.

   > You are the only person on earth who can use your abilities (Rick Warren)

   > Gifts reveal the character of those who receive them. (Mike Murdock)

3. I stumbled on an article by Professor Reno, a theologian. He had read a recent book written by a brain scientist on

the relationship between the brain and the behavior of a human specimen. Here are some extracts from the article.

> We often hear that modern science requires us to reject traditional Christian views of the human person. The argument goes something like this: If we can see the physical process by which ideas are associated or feelings felt or decisions made, then surely we must admit that human beings are nothing more than physical entities. The concept of a soul, so we are told, is irrelevant.
>
> Well, it turns out that science now points us in a different direction. These days, cognitive scientists are doing experiments that use MRI technology to visualize the brain while subjects undergo experiences, solve problems, and make decisions. This approach allows scientists to see and theorize about the significance and sources of patterns in our brains, patterns that shape the way we respond to the world. We are learning about the highway system of neurological movement, which turns out to be decisive for the way our minds work.
>
> The new emphasis on patterns of neural activity suggests an important support for the traditional Christian understanding of the soul. The cutting edge of brain science makes it clear that it is as foolish to say that our brains are just neurons as it is to say that highways are just concrete and asphalt. After all, what matters to the motorist is the way in which the concrete is organized to create an interlocking system of usable roads. The same holds for the gray matter inside our heads. The Christian tradition has long taught the same thing about the human person. St. Thomas drew on Aristotle's philosophy to define the soul as the form of the body. The soul is the pattern or

> highway system that organizes our bodies, including, of course, our brains.
>
> What's striking, however, is that the new scientific work on the brain offers an even more interesting and dramatic confirmation of traditional views of the soul. In a recent MRI study, "The Vulcanization of the Human Brain: A Neural Perspective on Interactions Between Cognition and Emotion," Princeton brain scientist Jonathan D. Cohen has looked at patterns of brain activity while subjects respond to moral dilemmas and make moral decisions. It turns out that the brain patterns related to moral decisions need to be trained. The soul must be disciplined.

This is quite interesting, and even more interesting to imagine that as a Christian, the Holy Spirit dwells in my nervous system.

DEMONIC STATE

In Figure 4.2, we see that satan is lobbying the body and the soul to get into the soul of the unregenerate. The soul is constantly involved in a struggle to choose between the promptings of the *universal grace* and the promptings of satan through various methods listed in Table 4.1. When satan attacks, either through [Emotion, Heart] or [Mind, Intellect], the processing of information is complex to say precisely what happens, but it seems that all the faculties get involved and Will takes the final decision which is passed through Heart or Emotion to the body. It is a battle between universal grace and the promptings of satan to win the soul of the unregenerate. The positive consideration of processing satan's signal by the soul is what Jesus calls "sin already committed" even before it is executed by the body (Matt 5: 28).

Extrinsic unclean spirits can only lodge in man's soul. The occupancy of the soul by the unclean spirits is what darkens the soul; these spirits can also bring thousands of their own elements and disrupt the order of the soul's network. Unclean spirits gain access into the soul by the permission of the Will. It is possible for satan to read one's mind if he gains entrance through his devils or demons to the soul. Otherwise, satan is not able to read the mind of a man.

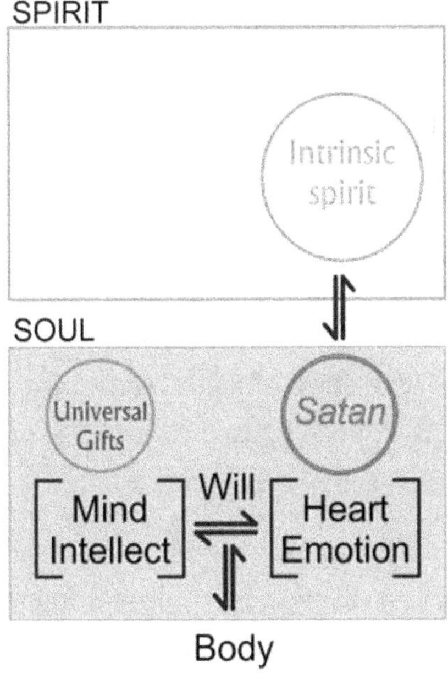

Figure 4.3: Triune State of Demonic Man

The popular attack methods satan uses to infiltrate into the soul of man are given in Table 4.1. There are of course more methods than those given. If satan manages to gain entrance into the soul, the triune state of the man is shown in Figure 4.3. To get him out of the soul, only God can do that as explained previously, perhaps through deliverance.

Being a spirit, the extrinsic unclean spirits should be able to communicate with the intrinsic spirit as shown in the Figure; however, that is not verified. As we compared the elements in the soul to neurons, spiritual universal gifts as well could run in the millions. The unclean spirits stain the soul. It is possible they also interfere with the universal gifts and really mess up the soul. The soul may be destroyed by these viruses as they may also interfere with the network and participate in the decision making processes of the Will. That is why God in the Old Testament, was always in anger when men let satan to mess up His good work.

Each of the spiritual universal gifts or unclean spirits in the soul may be qualified by the name of the element, for example, spirit of fear, spirit of anger, spirit of wisdom.

> For God hath not given us the spirit of fear; but of power, and of love, and of a sound mind. 2 Tim. 1: 7

God, through universal grace, assigns spiritual gifts to each of the faculties; satan also has spiritual agents assigned to each of the faculties as indicated in Table 4.1.

Emotion is the easiest faculty satan can attack and the Will is the most difficult for satan, being the strongest. Once the Will gives in, you can be sure that the whole network is in danger. The body responds to emotional decisions faster than any other. Attacks on emotions can sometimes lead to suicide. All the three satan's attacks (temptations) of Jesus, at the start of His ministry, were emotional. We have also seen that the spirit is also emotional. God Himself is compassionate; God is love.

REGENERATE STATE

Before regeneration, satan battles the universal grace for the soul as shown in Figure 4.2 and wins the soul in Figure 4.3. It is easier to regenerate the soul of Figure 4.2 than that of Figure 4.3 that has already been occupied by satanic agents. Regeneration takes place when someone gives his life to Christ and receives salvation.

Process of Regeneration

The Holy Spirit resides in the regenerated soul.

> But if the Spirit of him that raised up Jesus from the dead dwell in you, he that raised up Christ from the dead shall also quicken your mortal bodies by his Spirit that dwelleth in you. Rom 8:11

> Ye are of God, little children, and have overcome them: because greater is he that is in you, than he that is in the world. 1 John 4: 4

If the soul is already occupied by satan, the first thing the Holy Spirit does is to dislodge him. After, the intrinsic spirit is changed completely (renewed) and the Heart is cleansed for the Holy Spirit to reside there.

> And I will give them one heart, and I will put a new spirit within you; and I will take the stony heart out of their flesh, and will give them an heart of flesh: Ezek. 11: 19

> Create in me a clean heart, O God; and renew a right spirit within me. Ps. 51: 10

The Holy Spirit resides in the Heart because there is where the life element of the soul is and there is where the intrinsic spirit communicates with. We see in Figures 4.4 and 4.5 that the soul receives initial general cleansing by the Holy Spirit.

> ... but ye are washed, but ye are sanctified, but ye are justified in the name of the Lord Jesus, and by the Spirit of our God (1 Cor. 6:11)

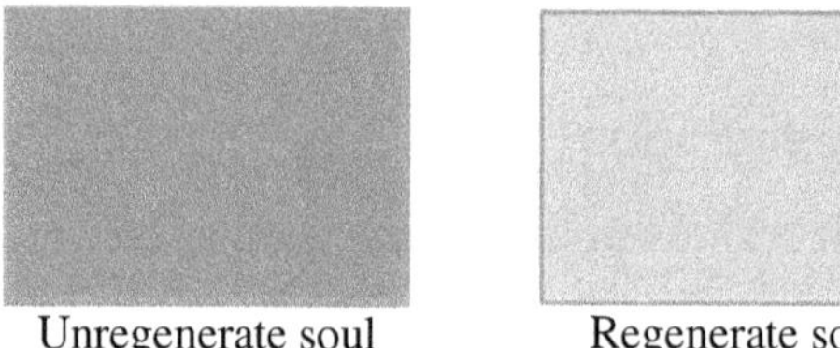

Figure 4.4: Soul before and after regeneration

The purpose of the Holy Spirit residing in the Heart is to be able to communicate with the regenerated soul and gradually remove the stains in the soul (a process called sanctification).

> Seeing ye have purified your souls in obeying the truth through the Spirit unto unfeigned love of the brethren,

see that ye love one another with a pure heart fervently: I Pet. 1: 22

But as it is written, Eye hath not seen, nor ear heard, neither have entered into the heart of man, the things which God hath prepared for them that love him. 1 Cor 2:9

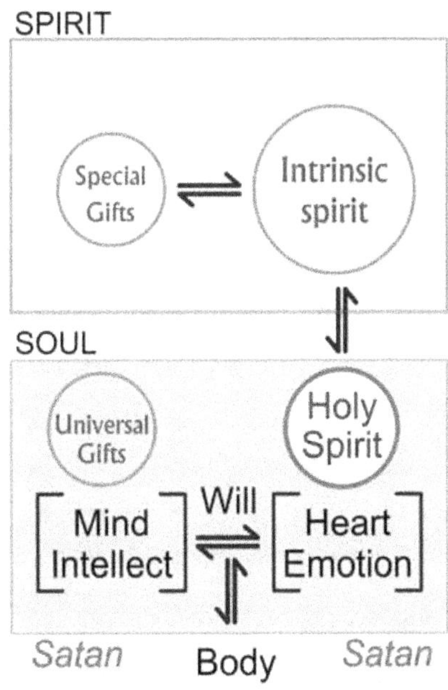

Figure 4.5: Triune State of Regenerate Man

Spiritual Special Gifts

In order to increase the strength of fellowship with the Holy Spirit residing in the soul, the spiritual frame may receive several *spiritual special gifts* (also quanta) at various energy levels depending on the measure of faith (Rom. 12:3). This is illustrated in Figure 4.5. The spiritual special gifts are clean and holy and assist the intrinsic spirit in the fellowship with God and the knowledge of Jesus (Eph. 4:13). Also, satan never gives up, he continues to lobby from outside the soul, but a strong believer will not respond to his promptings. The spiritual special gifts also help to recharge the intrinsic spirit.

Holy Spirit

The Spirit of God dwells in the heart also to prevent any unclean spirit to pick up residence there. The mind and intellect are gradually developed through the teaching and searching of the Holy Spirit. The problem a believer might face is how to separate the instructions of the Holy Spirit from the whisperings of satan. We can identify the work of the Holy Spirit in the five fingers of soul.

Heart

> For the law of the Spirit of life in Christ Jesus hath made me free from the law of sin and death. Rom. 8:2
>
> Who hath also sealed us, and given the earnest of the Spirit in our hearts. 2 Cor 1: 22
>
> Let the word of Christ dwell in you richly in all wisdom; teaching and admonishing one another in psalms and hymns and spiritual songs, singing with grace in your hearts to the Lord. Col 3:16

Intellect

> That in every thing ye are enriched by him, in all utterance, and in all knowledge; 1 Cor 1:5

But God hath revealed them unto us by his Spirit: for the Spirit searcheth all things, yea, the deep things of God. 1 Cor. 2: 10

And thou shalt speak unto all that are wise hearted, whom I have filled with the spirit of wisdom, that they may make Aaron's garments to consecrate him, that he may minister unto me in the priest's office. Exo 28: 3

Mind

And he that searcheth the hearts knoweth what is the mind of the Spirit, because he maketh intercession for the saints according to the Will of God. Rom. 8: 27

For God hath not given us the spirit of fear; but of power, and of love, and of a sound mind. 2 Tim. 1: 7

Will

Finally, my brethren, be strong in the Lord, and in the power of his might. Eph. 6: 10

Emotion

This I say then, Walk in the Spirit, and ye shall not fulfil the lust of the flesh. For the flesh lusteth against the Spirit, and the Spirit against the flesh: and these are contrary the one to the other: so that ye cannot do the things that ye would. Gal 5:16-17

Do ye think that the scripture saith in vain, The spirit that dwelleth in us lusteth to envy? James 4: 5

With both soul and spirit renewed, your body now becomes the temple of God because the Holy Spirit takes control of both thc spiritual frame and the soul.

Responsibility of Soul

After regeneration, the soul still remains the mediator between the body and the spirits, and will now be constantly involved in a struggle to choose between the promptings of the Holy Spirit and the promptings of the carnal flesh because satan never gives up. The Spirit of the living God within the person, must become manifested enough to win the battle for the soul.

> Dearly beloved, I beseech you as strangers and pilgrims, abstain from fleshly lusts, which war against the soul;
> 1 Pet 2: 11

SECURITY OF SALVATION

Can man really forfeit his salvation? The answer is yes. Satan has no power to dislodge the Holy Spirit that resides in the Heart unless the Holy Spirit voluntarily leaves. That is why Solomon (from his experience) writes several times, "do not vex the Holy Spirit". Gospel of salvation is connecting to God through Jesus Christ, the first Great Commandment (see Chapters 7 and 8). The only thing that can take salvation away is losing that connection, that is, apostasy. Other sins, such as adultery, murder, and so on, are from disobeying the second Great Commandment, the Gospel of works; they cannot make man to forfeit salvation but can only cut man off from entrance into the Kingdom of God (see Chapter 9). Apostasy can occur if the soul repeatedly fails to yield to the universal grace or teaching of the resident Holy Spirit. This can happen to someone who is impatient for the complete removal of his hard stains.

The Holy Spirit dwelling in the heart is the symbol of Salvation. Salvation is not lost unless the Holy Spirit vacates the Heart and the intrinsic spirit can no longer communicate with God; that was why David prayed strongly:

> Cast me not away from thy presence; and take not thy Holy Spirit from me. Restore unto me the joy of thy salvation; and uphold me with thy free Spirit (Ps. 51:11-12)

Perpetual sin of idolatry without repentance will make the Holy Spirit vacate.

> No man can serve two masters: for either he will hate the one, and love the other; or else he will hold to the one, and despise the other. Ye cannot serve God and mammon. (Matt. 6: 24; Luke 16:13)

SANCTIFIED STATE

Sanctification is the process of renewing man's soul towards perfection. After regeneration, the Holy Spirit resides in the soul to begin the cleansing, removing the evil elements.

Important things to know about sanctification:

1. Regeneration must come before sanctification;
2. The Holy Spirit has to remain in the soul. He must not depart the soul; otherwise it is begin-again;
3. Regeneration is an immediate event while sanctification takes place gradually;

4. Sanctification is not complete until the soul is *Adamic* or Christ-like.

Regenerate soul before sanctification

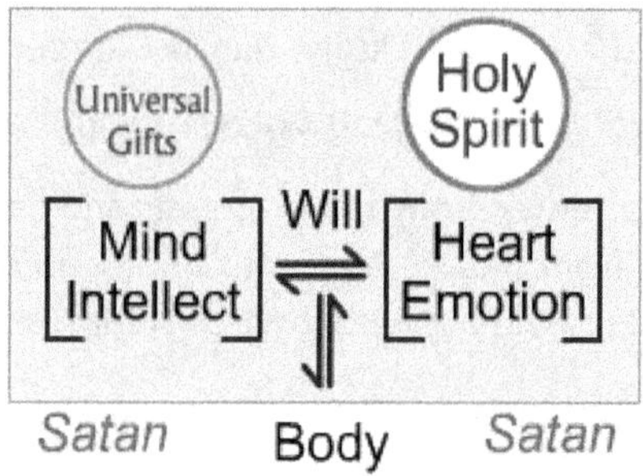

Gradual purification of soul until a few gray spots is left

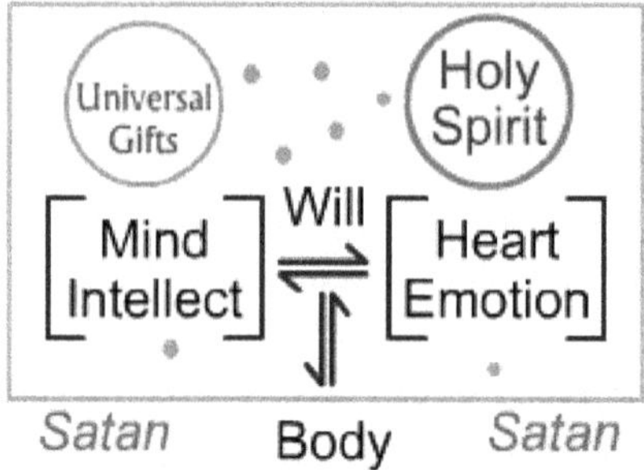

Figure 4.5: The Sanctification of Regenerate soul

Can the soul ever be Adamic? Is it really possible to achieve perfection? John Wesley says it is possible. Theoretically yes, but actually it is difficult. However, Noah and Job were perfect in their generations.

5. GOD

WHO can totally figure God out? I remember a joke in high school days about a student who had failed to study for a test in Bible Knowledge; one of the test questions was: *can you briefly describe what you know about the life and ministry of Jesus?* This student did not waste time to write down his one-liner answer: *Who am I to write about my Lord Jesus?* Of course, we can guess what the student scored in the test.

Anyway, what else can one write about God with volumes of literature on Him? Many people seem to be experts on the subject. However, I find exception in some writings about God that look presumptuous.

THE WILL OF GOD

Theologians generally write that God's Will is in two parts; most of them classify God's Will as follows:

- Decretive Will: describes *decrees* of things in which God has positively fore-ordained.
- Permissive Will: describes the things which God allows to exist or happen.

The permissive Will is not a Will per se from the definition. Calvinists prefer to classify God's Will as "*hidden*" and "*revealed*" (Pink). Calvinists claim that God decrees everything both good and evil; God decreed the fall of Adam even before he was created. Both classifications, theologians and Calvinists, serve their specific purposes. The theologians' classification is intended not to portray God as the author of evil although He allows it. The Calvinists' classification is intended to justify their doctrine of predestination, that God ordains everything both good and evil. To any reader, both might make sense, but each has its strength and weakness. Let us go through some points.

1. God has only one Will and it is not hidden; He created man in His own image. That we do not fully understand Him does not make Him to have different Wills. If any part of God's Will is hidden (as classified by Calvinists), then Jesus would not have said that one needs to do the Will of God by doing His Commandments to receive eternal life (Matt 7:21, Matt 19:17, Rev. 22:17). What theologians and Calvinist Pink have classified is the *Plan*

of God. There is a difference between *Plan* and *Will.* Paul writes about the "*hidden wisdom*" of God in 1 Cor. 2:7. The Application Study Bible interprets this as the "*hidden plan*" of God to offer Jesus for our salvation. There are *revealed plans* and *unrevealed plans* of God. The Will of God is known and that is the two Great Commandments (the Gospel of God in two parts). Jesus says nobody can have eternal life without doing the Will of the Father. The Will of God is not "hidden" otherwise Jesus would not be asking man to do God's Will.

2. God's Will is for man to have a good relationship with Him and for men to have good relationships with each other (1 Thess 4:3-9)
3. God is not evil and cannot decree evil to happen. Throughout the scripture, we read about different attributes of God, His loving kindness, His goodness, His compassion, and so on. It is a mistaken identity by thinking that He foreordains evil just because we cannot understand why He sometimes let evil happen. God foreknows, but He does not foreordain evil. Let us examine the case of Judas Iscariot for example. Jesus knew him before he was chosen so that the scripture might be fulfilled. Jesus never said that Judas was purposely created for that. It was not God that hardened him; it was satan (Luke 22:3, 4). God foreknew that it would happen.
4. God ensures that His purpose of creation materializes and it is not thwarted. Yes, He sometimes uses evil as an

instrument to ensure that His purpose is not thwarted by enemies or any event; that doesn't make Him evil.

On Adam's disobedience, Pink wrote:

> That God had decreed sin should enter this world through the disobedience of our first parents was a secret hid in His own breast. Of this Adam knew nothing, and that made all the difference so far as his responsibility was concerned. Adam was quite unacquainted with the Creator's hidden counsels. What concerned him was God's revealed will.

That God purposely made man to sin so that His Will is accomplished is not tenable. It makes God a joker.

THE DECREES OF GOD

The Decrees of God is defined as:

> His eternal purpose, according to the counsel of His will, whereby, for His own glory, he hath fore-ordained whatsoever comes to pass" (Willard 1690).

In the 55 verses of its occurrence in the scripture, the word "decree" is mainly used for Kings making declarations. It is not directly used for God's declarations. One of the supporting verses, Psalm 2:7, cited by Arthur Pink in "*The Attributes of God*", actually refers to King David's decree.

> I will declare the decree: the LORD hath said unto me, Thou art my Son; this day have I begotten thee. Ps. 2:7

The Decrees of God is a Reformed theology. One of the favorite verses quoted by predestinarians is:

> Declaring the end from the beginning, and from ancient times the things that are not yet done, saying, My counsel shall stand, and I will do all my pleasure: Isaiah 46:10

From this verse, the predestinarians use the word "decree" indiscriminately, God decrees this, and God decrees that! The Westminster Confession of Faith (1643) states:

> By the decree of God, for the manifestation of his glory, some men and angels are predestinated unto everlasting life, and others foreordained to everlasting death.

John Calvin wrote in his *Institutes of Christian Religion*:

> God saves whom he wills of his mere good pleasure... It was his good pleasure to doom [the lost] to destruction...

Isaiah 46:10 is being misused by these predestinarians. How can they say that it is the pleasure of God to predestinate some to Hell? God has no pleasure in punishing anyone. His words to this effect were recorded by Ezekiel:

> Have I any pleasure in the death of the wicked? saith the Lord Jehovah; and not rather that he should return from his way, and live?... I have no pleasure in the death of him that dieth, saith the Lord Jehovah Eze. 18:23,32.

So who do we believe, God or these predestinarian preachers? More on this will be covered in Chapter 10.

THE SOVEREIGNTY OF GOD

DEFINITION

Sovereignty of God means that He has absolute authority over all His creatures and He has created all things (Gen. 1:1). This sovereignty of God over everything including time is foundational. No one can challenge His decisions.

> And all the inhabitants of the earth are reputed as nothing: and He doeth according to His will in the army of Heaven, and among the inhabitants of the earth: and none can stay His hand, or say unto Him, what doest Thou? Dan. 4:35.

> Declaring the end from the beginning, and from ancient times the things that are not yet done, saying, My counsel shall stand, and I will do all my pleasure: Isa 46: 10

He rules over the Heavens and earth. He alone determines the appropriate course of action.

> But our God is in Heavens: He hath done whatsoever He hath pleased. Ps. 115:3

> For the Kingdom is the Lord's: and he is the governor among the nations. Ps 22:28

> The earth is the Lord's, and the fullness thereof; the world, and they that dwell therein. Ps. 24:1

Arthur Pink defines God's sovereignty as follows:

> The sovereignty of God may be defined as the exercise of His supremacy. Being infinitely elevated above the high-

> est creature, He is the Most High, Lord of Heaven and earth. Subject to none, influenced by none, absolutely independent; God does as He pleases, only as He pleases always as He pleases. None can thwart Him, none can hinder Him. (Pink)

God is infinite and man is finite, man will never be able to understand Him completely. He uses even the activities of the wicked and evil spirits for His good purposes.

> The Lord hath made all things for Himself: yea, even the wicked for the day of evil. Prov. 16:4

> But the spirit of the Lord departed from Saul, and an evil spirit from the Lord troubled him. 1 Sam 16:14

> Then God sent an evil spirit between Abimelech and the men of Shechem; and the men of Shechem dealt treacherously with Abimelech. Judges 9:23

God is sovereign in His mercy and His grace.

> And he said, I will make all my goodness pass before thee, and I will proclaim the name of the Lord before thee; and will be gracious to whom I will be gracious, and will shew mercy on whom I will shew mercy.
> Exo. 33: 19

SOVEREIGN ATTRIBUTES OF GOD

Eternal

God is eternal means He is everlasting; He has no beginning and no ending either. God created time as we know it, He lives outside of time and He knows and can see the beginning and the end of time.

> And Abraham planted a grove in Beersheba, and called there on the name of the Lord, the everlasting God.
> Gen 21:33

> The eternal God is thy refuge, and underneath are the everlasting arms: and he shall thrust out the enemy from before thee; and shall say, Destroy them. Deut 33: 27

> Blessed be the Lord God of Israel from everlasting, and to everlasting. Amen, and Amen. Ps 41: 13

> Hast thou not known? hast thou not heard, that the everlasting God, the Lord, the Creator of the ends of the earth, fainteth not, neither is weary? there is no searching of his understanding. Is 40: 28

God has always existed and He always will. Nothing can ever be able to bring an end to Him.

Omnipresence

God is omnipresent means He fills the entire universe and He has the ability to be everywhere at one time.

> The LORD looketh from heaven; he beholdeth all the sons of men. Ps. 33:13

> Whither shall I go from thy Spirit? Or whither shall I flee from thy presence? If I ascend up into Heaven, thou art there: if I make my bed in hell, behold, thou art there.
> Ps 139 7-8

> Am I a God at hand, saith the Lord, and not a God afar off? Can any hide himself in secret places that I shall not

> see him? saith the Lord. Do not I fill Heaven and earth? saith the Lord. Jer 23:23-24

No one can hide from God. There is no where to go where He is not.

Omniscience

God is omniscient means He has all knowledge; He knows everything infinitely. God knows everything that has happened and everything that will happen. He perfectly and eternally knows all things which can be known, past, present, and future. Like omnipresence, man cannot hide from God because He knows all things, including minute details. He knows the number of hairs on each head; He knows the thoughts and feelings of every man. When no man is around to see our wrong-doing, God is.

> Dost thou know the balancings of the cloud, the wondrous works of Him which is perfect in knowledge? Job 37:16

> The Lord looketh from Heaven; he beholdeth all the sons of men. Psalm 33:13

> He telleth the number of the stars; he calleth them all by their names. Great is our Lord, and of great power: his understanding is infinite. Ps 147:4-5

> Known to God are all his works from the beginning of the world. Acts 15:18

In 2 Kings 6:8-11, the King of Syria was surprised that the King of Israel knew he was going to hide at a certain place. The King of Israel did not know, but God knew.

Omnipotence

God is omnipotent means that He is all-powerful. He has the ability to do whatever He wills. If God says something will happen, He has the power to make sure that it will happen. To a certain extent, He has voluntarily limited Himself by the free will of His rational creatures.

> Thine, O Lord, is the greatness, and the power, and the glory, and the victory, and the majesty: for all that is in the Heaven and in the earth is thine; thine is the Kingdom, O Lord, and thou art exalted as the head above all. Both riches and honour come of thee, and thou reignest over all; and in thine hand is power and might; and in thine hand it is to make great, and to give strength unto all. 1 Chr. 29:11-12

> Let every soul be subject unto the higher powers. For there is no power but of God: the powers that be are ordained of God. Rom 13: 1

> But Jesus beheld them, and said unto them, With men this is impossible; but with God all things are possible. Matt 19:26

> I know that thou canst do everything, and that no thought can be withholden from thee. Job 42:2

> Behold, I am the Lord, the God of all flesh: is there any thing too hard for me? Jer 32:27

> For with God nothing shall be impossible. Luke 1:37

DISCUSSION

Philosophers and atheists have debated theologians on these attributes of God, especially the possibility of God to be omnipotent and omniscient at the same time. The argument that divine foreknowledge is not compatible with free will is known as *fatalism*. A "fatalist" would say "*OK, if God has already decided everything that will happen, then why should I do anything? He controls history anyway. Therefore, we can just sit back and do nothing.*" These debates are pursued with human wisdom and rationality. It suffices to say that God's ways are not our ways and with God, nothing is impossible.

God's sovereignty is unquestionable for we are nothing (Dan 4:35); however, events in the scripture also show that our God is emotional.

> And it repented the Lord that He had made man on earth, and it grieved Him at His heart. Gen. 6:6

It would seem that God voluntarily lowers Himself to be able to fellowship with man. God has heart. God definitely has the ability to decree every event in the future, but it seems He chooses not to. He has declared what the future should be in a global perspective and He works to ensure that His plans are not thwarted. It grieves God when man sins. He could not have decreed that Sodom would sink in sin and later come down to destroy the people of Sodom. He leaves us to our Will.

With the gift of time, God allows us to participate in his sovereignty as we use our time to trust him from the beginning of our lives, each day of our lives, and in the future of our lives. (DeVries)

6. TIMELINE OF GRACE

IN this Chapter, we will try to determine the timeline of the plan of salvation through the special grace. We will also determine when God instituted the universal grace.

Before Jesus came to the world, mankind depended only on the universal grace of God. Early grace theologians concentrated on the New Testament and as such could not think of the universal grace. The New Testament was written after Jesus came; so Paul and other writers focused on the saving grace of Jesus. But universal grace was what kept man before Jesus came; so we have to research the Old Testament to understand the origin of universal grace (and even of special grace). In the Old Testament, the word "grace" appears in 38 verses and most of the usages signify "favor". Divine favor is one of the manifestations of universal grace, as covered in Chapter 3. The manifestation of *universal grace*, as gifts, occurs at different stages in the history of mankind. Unlike universal grace, special grace of salvation was systematically planned. Such a planned event takes place in three stages:

1. *Planning or Conception*;
2. *Validation of Plan*;
3. *Actualization.*

We will study the timeline for the manifestations of grace.

PLANNING

Before man was created, the gift of earth and its riches, by God's universal grace, was already established. Also, as discussed in Chapter 4 (under "Will of Man"), it is suggested that before the creation of man, satan challenged God; because of this, the all-knowing God foresaw the fall of man and set the plan of salvation in motion. Jesus offered Himself for the propitiation of sin. Various verses in the scripture confirm that the death of Jesus for the propitiation of man's sins was planned before the creation of man.

> For then must he often have suffered since the foundation of the world: but now once in the end of the world hath he appeared to put away sin by the sacrifice of himself. Heb 9: 26

> Who verily was foreordained before the foundation of the world, but was manifest in these last times for you, 1 Pet 1: 20

> And all that dwell upon the earth shall worship him, whose names are not written in the book of life of the Lamb slain from the foundation of the world. Rev 13: 8

The implication of the sacrifice of Jesus and the planning of special grace is discussed in Chapter 7. I will offer an opinion on the validation of the plan for special grace. As discussed in Chapters 3 and 4, Adam was created with some spiritual universal gifts; but those do not assist man not to sin. Critical moments in the history of man will help in understanding the timeline of validation of grace. Validation here means when God decided to go with the plan.

CRITICAL MOMENTS

There are three critical moments in the early history of man that necessitated God's intervention. These moments will help in the understanding of the timelines of both universal and special grace.

FIRST: MAN SINS

God initially created the earth as one of His Kingdoms and wanted man to rule over it pending the time Jesus would come. God created man with a latent power, "Will", for two purposes, as discussed in Chapter 4. Also, there was only one commandment for Adam not to eat from the tree of discernment, but Adam flouted it in spite of his understanding of the consequences well spelt out. The commandment was given to Adam before Eve was created, so Adam bears the guilt of the sin committed. God got disappointed because of man's fall. He visited the garden and sent Adam and his wife away with curses. This was the first critical moment in the history of man, a very important one; man's Will was corrupted. Man got separated from the *tree of life* and can not live eternally. Sin brought death. It was at this moment Jesus' offer to sacrifice Himself for permanent atonement of sin, was first *validated.* For temporary atonement, God demanded for repeated sin offerings.

Even with the temporary atonement, the first child on earth sinned, indicating that Adam's sin has put man in a state of depravity and not able not to sin. Then, man had no *conscience*; when Cain sinned he asked: "Am I my brother's keeper"? After repeating Cain's sin, Lamech also showed no remorse (Gen. 4:23-24). The first critical moment on earth was therefore man's sin. Man did not know how to repent.

SECOND: GOD INSTITUTES UNIVERSAL GRACE

As the earth was being populated, men soon forgot about God's sin offering and sin multiplied. Initially, God was always getting angry at the collective sins of men.

> And God saw that the wickedness of man was great in the earth, and that every imagination of the thoughts of his heart was only evil continually (Gen. 6:5)

The passage above shows that God is not the author of wickedness and evil thoughts, even though He is the Creator of the carrier (Prov. 16:4).

> And it repented the Lord that He had made man on earth, and it grieved Him at His heart. And the Lord said, I will destroy man whom I have created from the face of the earth; both man, and the beast, and the creeping thing, and the fowls of the air; for it repenteth Me that I have made them Gen. 6:6-7

Adam's transmitted sin on earth is very devastating to the extent that God regretted creating everything and wanted to destroy them. In His anger, He destroyed men by flood (Gen. 6) but kept Noah and his family and the term "grace" appears for the first time in the Bible (KJV).

> But Noah found grace in the eyes of the Lord (Gen 6: 8)

Noah was the first man after the flood to receive salvation. Noah was a just and perfect man for that generation (Gen. 6:9) and God felt He could rebuild the earth with him and his family. After the flood, God made a covenant (Gen. 9:8-17) that He would not destroy man by flood again. The specificity of using flood was because that was the method available to Him then and it was still fresh. The covenant God was making is that He would not destroy the totality of His creation anymore. Some discussions must have transpired in Heaven for God to make such a covenant. God has just destroyed almost all His six days work; in anger! However, He decided to make the covenant and to relax His curse over the earth and instituted a *universal gift of life* and some *spiritual universal gifts*, through His Spirit to protect and preserve life and to assist the "Will" of man in making good choices.

> Whosoever sheddeth man's blood, by man shall his blood be shed: for in the image of God made He man. And you, be ye fruitful, and multiply; bring forth abundantly in the earth, and multiply therein. (Gen. 9:6-7)

God's spiritual gifts through the universal grace, then, resides in man's soul to work on conscience, emotion, intellect and to assist man's Will in making good choices. Kuyper, in "*Calvinism and Politics*", disappointedly saw the issue of the covenant with a different eyeglass; he used it to help Calvinists defend the institution of capital punishment:

> Luther and his co-Reformers have correctly pointed out that the institution proper and the full investiture of the magistrate with power were only brought about after the flood, when God commanded that capital punishment should fall upon him who shed man's blood. The right of taking life belongs only to Him. who can give life, i.e., to God; and therefore no one on earth is invested with this authority, except it be God-given (Kuyper)

Rousas Rushdoony may have picked up from there to start his *Reconstructionism* in the 1970s. However, the covenant is a milestone in the institution of universal grace to assist man's Will. With the universal grace, sin seized to become a reason for total annihilation of mankind. That was the second critical period on earth – the flood and the covenant.

> But God arrested sin in its course in order to prevent the complete annihilation of His divine handiwork, which naturally would have followed. He has interfered in the

> life of the individual, in the life of mankind as a whole, and in the life of nature itself by His common grace. This grace, however, does not kill the core of sin, nor does it save unto life eternal, but it arrests the complete effectuation of sin, just as human insight arrests the fury of wild beasts. (Kuyper)

After having written this Chapter, the Holy Spirit led me to read the verses below.

> By which also he went and preached unto the spirits in prison; Which sometime were disobedient, when once the longsuffering of God waited in the days of Noah, while the ark was a preparing, wherein few, that is, eight souls were saved by water. The like figure whereunto even baptism doth also now save us (not the putting away of the filth of the flesh, but the answer of a good conscience toward God,) by the resurrection of Jesus Christ: 1 Pet 3: 19-21

These difficult passages have received various interpretations. However, we know that in the passages, Peter focuses on two great judgments:

1) the judgment of Noah's day and
2) the judgment of fallen angels.

Peter seems to be saying that there was an account to settle during the event of the flood that Jesus did between His death and resurrection. This shows that Jesus has been active in Heavenly decisions since creation and the event of the flood was a critical moment.

THIRD: GOD REVALIDATES SPECIAL GRACE

After the flood and repopulation of the earth, men began to think too highly of themselves, building a tower to reach Heaven and continuing in sin. God decided to start afresh again; this time He selected a people among the people of the earth (Is. 44:1) that He would develop to be His own (Is. 43:1, 21) and that He would through them show the earth He is the only true God (Rom. 9:17). Through these people, He would build a Holy Kingdom (Exo. 19:5-6) and the earth would learn how to worship Him. He selected Abraham to build this nation.

The third critical moment on earth came when three Heaven emissaries had to come down. It seemed that man was irredeemable. The sins in Sodom and Gomorrah made Heaven uncomfortable; it was the peak of sin and immorality on earth. God in anger once again destroyed men collectively by rain of brimstone, not the entire creation because of His covenant, but Sodom and Gomorrah (Gen. 19); the angels spared Lot's life and the term "grace" appears the second time in the Bible:

> Behold, now thy servant hath found grace in thy sight, and thou hast magnified thy mercy, which thou hast shewed unto me in saving my life; and I cannot escape to the mountain, lest some evil take me, and I die.
> Gen. 19:19

The first two times the term "grace" appears in the Bible (KJV) are in reference to saving lives, first of Noah, then of

Lot, during two critical moments on earth. It could be coincidental, but it is worth noting.

One of the emissaries who visited Abraham in Genesis 18 before the destruction of Sodom could have been Jesus. In response to some enquiring Jews, Jesus said:

> Your father Abraham rejoiced to see my day: and he saw it, and was glad. John 8: 56

How did Abraham see Jesus? If we study the follow up of the passage where Jesus clearly describes his pre-existence as deity before Abraham, then most likely Jesus was talking about that physical visit of Genesis 18:

> Then said the Jews unto him, Thou art not yet fifty years old, and hast thou seen Abraham? Jesus said unto them, Verily, verily, I say unto you, Before Abraham was, I am. John 8: 57-58

However, for Heaven to come down to earth, another serious discussion must have transpired in Heaven for the second time. Most likely, it was at this moment (before or after the destruction of Sodom) that God finally revalidated his plan of salvation that Jesus would come first to the earth for permanent atonement, hence the confirmation of His *special grace to* mankind. Note that God still wanted to destroy the entire world after His first validation (after Adam sinned). Atonement will be further discussed later in Chapter 7. It is also worth noting that the lineage that God selected disappointed Him with their "stiffneck" attitude during their wandering in the wilderness; God wanted to wipe them out and to once again rebuild with Moses (Deut. 10:13-14). God can not stand sin and therefore permanent atonement (propitiation) was absolutely necessary.

DISCUSSION

SUMMARY OF TIMELINE

The timeline of the manifestation of God's grace is summarized in Table 6.1.

Table 6.1: Timeline of Grace of God

Event	**Universal Gifts**	**Special Grace**
Before the creation of man	Material (Earth, etc)	Planned
At the creation of Adam	spiritual	
After Adam sinned		Validated
After the flood	Life, spiritual, favor, restraint	
After destruction of Sodom and Gomorrah		Revalidated
On the cross of Calvary		Actualized

WHY JESUS COMES SEVERAL TIMES

At creation, Jesus was with God and God had slated Jesus to come and take over the rulership of the earth's Kingdom (Col. 1:13-17; Rev. 3:14) from the self-imposed devil.

> I will put enmity between thee and the woman and between thy seed and her seed... (Gen. 2:15, Gal 4:4).

> In the beginning was the Word, and the Word was with God. John 1:1

> He that committeth sin is of the devil; for the devil sinneth from the beginning. For this purpose the Son of God was manifested, that he might destroy the works of the devil. I John 3: 8

> Then shall the King say unto them on his right hand, Come, ye blessed of my Father, inherit the Kingdom prepared for you from the foundation of the world: Matt 25: 34

It would seem that Jesus' coming was to be only once and for all. Because of man's sin, Jesus' initial offer was validated to first come as a perfect sacrifice before He finally returns for the rulership of His Kingdom on earth. Although God planned the permanent atonement by Christ Jesus at the beginning of creation, but it appears that He did not validate to send Jesus at that moment. The passages below suggest that Jesus was the one who volunteered to lay His life down for atonement. This self-giving is linked to the sacrificial ritual explicitly.

> I am the good shepherd: the good shepherd giveth his life for the sheep. John 10: 11

> As the Father knoweth me, even so know I the Father: and I lay down my life for the sheep. John 10: 15

> How much more shall the blood of Christ, who through the eternal Spirit offered himself without spot to God,

> purge your conscience from dead works to serve the living God? Heb 9: 14

The two verses below seem to show that Jesus volunteered to lay himself down before the foundation of the world.

> Therefore doth my Father love me, because I lay down my life, that I might take it again. John 10: 17

> For then must he often have suffered since the foundation of the world: but now once in the end of the world hath he appeared to put away sin by the sacrifice of himself. Heb 9: 26

Jesus says the Father loved Him before the foundation of the world and for laying down His life.

God regretted creating man in Gen. 6:6. It seems that God trusted His Kingdom on earth to be ruled by man before Jesus comes. But satan usurped God's authority on earth. The most likely time of God's final validation to send Jesus first for permanent atonement is before or after the destruction of Sodom and Gomorrah. After the destruction of the cities, the incident is cited severally (in 33 verses) in the Bible in reference to sin, abomination, judgment, and punishment. It is referenced by God, Jesus, Isaiah, Jeremiah, Ezekiel, Paul, Peter, Jude, and John in Revelation. Jesus has saved the world for Himself and He is coming back to take over His throne for eternity. Read Daniel 7:13-14.

7. DOCTRINE OF SALVATION

IN this Chapter, the doctrine of special grace will be elaborated. According to revelations discussed in *Missional Reformation* (Olowe 2009), and which will be discussed further in Chapter 8, the Gospel of Salvation (Gospel of special grace) is derived from the first Great Commandment (Deut. 6:5; Matt 22:37):

> Thou shalt love the Lord thy God with all thy heart, and with all thy soul, and with all thy mind.

Loving God connects us to God. Because of sin, man is not able to fellowship with God directly. In the Old Testament, the fellowship was made possible through regular sacrifices. The doctrine of salvation is to teach us how Jesus Christ made the connection to God possible without the need of the regular sacrifices of the Old Testament. After Jesus died on the cross, salvation can be received through Jesus Christ only. The goal of salvation is to obtain eternal life.

> That whosoever believeth in him should not perish, but have eternal life. John 3: 15

In order to understand and appreciate the death of Jesus, we will look at the origin of sacrifices in the Old Testament.

OLD TESTAMENT SACRIFICES

In the Old Testament, sacrifices allowed Israel to worship and be in a right relationship with God. Offerings and sacrifices were made to thank, to make a request, and to serve as a means to bring man to repentance. The laws God gave to Moses and the people called for a number of specific kinds of sacrifices or offerings.

PRE-ISRAEL SACRIFICES

Before the nation of Israel was established, there were sacrifices recorded during the patriarchal period; for example, Job's offering of animal sacrifices for the sins of his family (Job 1:5). The first account of sacrificing unto God by men dates back to the period of Cain and Abel, the first children on earth. Cain and Abel made sacrifices to the Lord, but Cain's sacrifice was rejected.

> And in process of time it came to pass, that Cain brought of the fruit of the ground an offering unto the Lord. And Abel, he also brought of the firstlings of his flock and of the fat thereof. And the Lord had respect unto Abel and to his offering: But unto Cain and to his offering he had not respect. And Cain was very wroth, and his countenance fell. Gen. 4: 3-5

The passages above raise two important questions since the scripture was silent about these. The questions are:

1. Where did Cain and Abel learn about sacrificing to remain right with God?
2. Why did God not respect Cain's sacrifice?

The response to the second question is important to help us understand why Jesus came to die for the sins of mankind.

Genesis of Sacrifice

After Adam and Eve sinned in the Garden, they covered their nakedness with leaves, but God made them "coats of skin" (Gen. 3:21). Many scholars of the Bible believe that a sacrifice was made before the coats of skin were made. Adam and Eve must have transferred the knowledge of sacrificing to their children.

Reason for Rejecting the Sacrifice of Cain

According to Hebrews 11:4, Abel's offering unto God was a "more excellent sacrifice". Why was Abel's sacrifice considered as more excellent? There are three possible reasons suggested among Bible scholars

1. Cain did not sacrifice his best harvest, the firstlings of his vegetables as Abel did of his flock. In order words, Cain's offering was below standard.
2. Some Bible scholars believe that Cain's bad and sinful life was not pleasing to God. This argument is weak because no where in the scripture is it mentioned or implied that Cain led a sinful life before he murdered his brother. Some other Bible scholars even argue that his crime arose not merely from jealousy, but from a desire to please the Lord.
3. Cain's offering of the fruit without a burnt offering was not acceptable. This is one view that supports and is consistent with the plan of redemption found in scripture. We see later that when the Lord wrote the law of sacrifices, in order to show devotion to God, or to ask for forgiveness, a life sacrifice is required. There was no shedding of blood in Cain's offering which is most likely the reason why God had no respect towards it. This argument also supports the first argument that Cain's offering was below God's standard.

SACRIFICES IN MOSAIC LAW

The book of Leviticus is one of the most important books of the Old Testament in Christianity. It lays the foundation of understanding the basis of salvation; it unfolds God's plan of redemption. The bulk of the book contains direct instructions from God that Moses delivered to the people. In the book of

Leviticus, God instituted sacrifice regulations for the nation of Israel. The sacrificial system served both as a means to worship and have fellowship with God. The rituals of the sacrifices (Lev. 1-7) enabled the sinful people to maintain fellowship with their covenant God. The consecrated priesthoods were to be the mediators between man and God to perform the rites (Lev. 8-10).

There were five different sacrifices which allowed the Israelites to have fellowship with God. The five sacrifices are given in Table 7.1 with their specific purposes. The objects offered for sacrifice are also given in the Table. The objects were sometimes brought by anybody, but only the priests could perform the sacrifices to be offered to the Lord.

Table 7.1: Sacrifices in worshiping God in the Mosaic Law

Sacrifice	Reason for Sacrifice	Sacrificial items	Leviticus Ref.
burnt offerings	To please the Lord. To show devotion to God, and to ask for God's forgiveness;	Bull, male sheep or goat without blemish, or a dove or pigeon for the poor. The entire object is burned	1:1-17; 6:8-13; 8:18-21; 16:23,24
grain offerings	To give thanks to the Lord; to recognize that God is the giver of blessings and provides good things	A mixture of fine wheat flour, olive oil and incense; bread baked without yeast or honey in loaves or wafers or fried in flat wafers; salt added sometimes; sometimes used along with burnt offerings or peace offerings	2:1-16; 6:14-23

Sacrifice	Reason for Sacrifice	Sacrificial items	Leviticus Ref.
peace offerings	To ask for God's blessing; some of the meat is kept and eaten (7.28-35)	Fat and certain inner organs from a bull, cow, sheep, or goat that has nothing wrong with it; various kinds of bread made without yeast	3:1-17; 7:11-36
sin offerings	To ask for God's forgiveness; to make amends for specific unintentional sins; to become clean after becoming ritually unclean	A young bull for the high priest and the whole nation; A male goat for a tribal leader; a female goat or lamb for ordinary people; two doves or pigeons for the poor; two pounds of fine flour for the very poor; two goats and a ram on the Great Day of Forgiveness (one goat carries the sins of the whole nation into the wilderness)	4:1--5:13; 6:24-30; 8:14-17; 16:3-22
guilt or trespass offerings	To make up for cheating the Lord or unintentionally destroying something that belonged to the Lord; to make up for robbing or cheating another person	A ram that has nothing wrong with it, or the price of the ram in addition to paying back what was stolen or destroyed plus twenty percent	5:14--6:7; 7:1-6

Adapted from American Bible Society (www.bibleresourcecenter.org)

The most common and important offerings were the sin and trespass offerings which were performed by the people to make atonement for sins committed unintentionally (Lev. 23: 27-32); they required animal sacrifices.

REASON FOR ANIMAL SACRIFICE

As discussed above, God made provision for the judicial price of sin to be paid by an animal.

> For the life of the flesh is in the blood: and I have given it to you upon the altar to make an atonement for your souls: for it is the blood that maketh an atonement for the soul. Lev 17: 11

We need to understand the importance and the reason for animal sacrifice (blood atonement) in the Old Testament era (from the Garden of Eden through the period of the patriarchs to the Mosaic Law), in other to comprehend the plan of redemption through Jesus Christ in the New Testament. God did not lust after the blood, but blood (which represents life) is the only thing that can atone for sin.

> And almost all things are by the law purged with blood; and without shedding of blood is no remission.
> Heb 9: 22

According to the scripture, Abel was the first man to offer animal sacrifice. After the flood, animal sacrifice was reestablished by Noah (Gen. 8:20-21). Abel must have learnt about animal sacrifices from Adam. When Adam and Eve sinned, they chose to cover their shame and guilt with leaves. But God made Adam and Eve "coats of skin" (Gen. 3:21). In the Scriptures, garments are sometimes used as symbols of righteousness.

> I will greatly rejoice in the Lord, my soul shall be joyful in my God; for he hath clothed me with the garments of salvation, he hath covered me with the robe of righteousness, as a bridegroom decketh himself with ornaments, and as a bride adorneth herself with her jewels. Isaiah 61: 10

> I put on righteousness, and it clothed me: my judgment was as a robe and a diadem. Job 29: 14

> He that overcometh, the same shall be clothed in white raiment; and I will not blot out his name out of the book of life, but I will confess his name before my Father, and before his angels. Rev. 3: 5

God covered Adam and Eve with the coats of skin that would make them to be able to stand in His holy presence. Since a life had to be sacrificed before Adam and Eve could have been clothed with "coats of sins", there was a substitutionary death. The sacrificial animal was most likely a lamb.

> And all that dwell upon the earth shall worship him, whose names are not written in the book of life of the Lamb slain from the foundation of the world. Rev 13: 8

The animal was innocent of sin; it couldn't sin, thereby qualifying it to be a substitute for the guilty sinner. Sinlessness was necessary to provide substitute death for the sinner. Mosaic Law explicitly mentions the requirements for a perfect, spotless and unblemished animal (Leviticus 22:21-27). Only male animals would be acceptable (Leviticus 22:19).

PROPITIATION

Propitiation is the removal of God's punishment for past sin through the perfect sacrifice of Jesus Christ.

> Herein is love, not that we loved God, but that he loved us, and sent his Son to be the propitiation for our sins. I John 4: 10

> And he is the propitiation for our sins: and not for ours only, but also for the sins of the whole world. I John 2: 2

> Whom God hath set forth to be a propitiation through faith in his blood, to declare his righteousness for the remission of sins that are past, through the forbearance of God; Rom 3: 25

The phrase "sins that are past" in Rom 3:25 is very important. This is what many believers omit in the interpretation of atonement. Jesus was sacrificed for only the sins that are past which includes the transmitted sins of Adam and our personal sins before receiving salvation. There is no amount of good works that can remove those sins from any man.

WHY JESUS WAS A PERFECT SACRIFICE

As we have discussed previously, a perfect sacrifice was necessary for the atonement of sin. Sinlessness was required for a substitute death for the sinner. In Chapter 4, it is shown that Jesus was the only man on earth without sin. Hence Jesus is the only human who could ever be accepted as a sacrifice. Animal sacrifices ended because Jesus Christ was the ultimate and perfect sacrifice.

> Who needeth not daily, as those high priests, to offer up sacrifice, first for his own sins, and then for the people's: for this he did once, when he offered up himself.
> Heb 7:27

> For the law having a shadow of good things to come, and not the very image of the things, can never with those sacrifices which they offered year by year continually make the comers thereunto perfect. Heb 10: 1

> But in those sacrifices there is a remembrance again made of sins every year. Heb 10: 3

> By the which will we are sanctified through the offering of the body of Jesus Christ once for all. Heb 10: 10

> For he hath made him to be sin for us, who knew no sin; that we might be made the righteousness of God in him.
> 2 Cor 5: 21

John the Baptist recognized this when Jesus approached him to be baptized; he said, "*Behold, the lamb of God which taketh away the sin of the world.*" (John 1:29).

ATONEMENT AND PROPITIATION

While *propitiation* describes better the work of Jesus on the cross to appease God's wrath permanently, *atonement* is used in the Old Testament to mean "to cover". Israel was required to offer the blood of an animal every year for the sins of the nation on the day of atonement (Exodus 30:10). The death of Jesus Christ was a *propitiation* for the sins of mankind not just a covering. The old repetitive system of atonement required under the Mosaic law was done away with once and for all in the new covenant with Jesus. The death of Jesus was the divinely intended fulfillment of the sacrificial rituals in the pre-Israel and post-Israel era; the death of Jesus was no ordinary death. Only in Christ is man ever properly clothed in righteousness and reconciled with God.

> For it is not possible that the blood of bulls and goats could take away sins. Heb 10:4

The word *atonement* will be used in this book to mean temporary relaxation of sin and *propitiation* will be used to describe Jesus' substitutionary death for the sins of mankind.

Christian groups understand *propitiation* in different ways; there are three major approaches: the *ransom* theory, the *satisfaction* theory and the *moral influence* theory.

1. The *ransom* approach is based on Mark 10:45, where Jesus says He gives his life as a ransom for many; this is taken to be a ransom to satan.
2. The *satisfaction* or *vicarious* approach on the other hand says that the blood of Jesus is paid as a debt to sovereign God Himself for human sins. Since the penalty for sin is death, someone had to pay for it; Jesus did. Penal substitution is a variation of this approach.
3. The *moral influence* theory is a more liberal approach; it maintains that Jesus' death on the cross was an example of God's love for mankind, not a form of blood sacrifice.

WHO JESUS DIED FOR

A cogent question about the sacrifice of Jesus that still lingers in the mind of believers is: who did Jesus die for? Calvinism teaches that Christ died for only a handful of mankind, called "the elect". But the Bible teaches quite clearly that Jesus Christ died for the sins of all people and wants all people to come to repentance.

> For since the beginning of the world men have not heard, nor perceived by the ear, neither hath the eye seen, O God, beside thee, what he hath prepared for him that waiteth for him. Isa. 64: 4
>
> For the son of man is come to save that which was lost. Matt. 18:11
>
> For God so loved the world, that He gave His only begotten Son, that whoever believes in Him should not perish, but have eternal life. (John 3:16)
>
> And I, if I be lifted up from the earth, will draw all men to Myself. (John 12:32)
>
> The Lord is not slow about His promise, as some count slowness, but is patient toward you, not wishing for any to perish but for all to come to repentance. (2 Pet. 3:9)
>
> For when we were yet without strength, in due time Christ died for the ungodly. Rom 5: 6
>
> For as in Adam all die, so also in Christ all shall be made alive. (1 Cor. 15:22)
>
> For the love of Christ controls us, having concluded this, that one died for all, therefore all died; and He died for all, that they who live should no longer live for them-

> selves, but for Him who died and rose again on their behalf. (2 Cor. 5:15)
>
> For it is for this we labor and strive, because we have fixed our hope on the living God, who is the Savior of all men, especially of believers. (1 Tim. 4:10)
>
> For the grace of God has appeared, bringing salvation to all men, (Titus 2:11)
>
> The Lord is not slack concerning his promise, as some men count slackness; but is longsuffering to us-ward, not willing that any should perish, but that all should come to repentance. 2Pet 3:9
>
> And He is the propitiation of our sins: not for ours only, but also for the sins of the whole world. 1 John 2:2

The above and several other passages show that permanent atonement (propitiation) is unlimited. Calvinists twist this last passage to prove that the "whole world" in John's statement means only "the elect scattered in the world". In trying to do so, Pink compared the passage with John 11:51-52 which specifically mentions "*He should gather together in one the children of God that were scattered abroad*". First of all, this was not Jesus' statement. It was a statement from Caiaphas, a high priest. Caiaphas could have been interpreting Jesus' statement in Matthew 24:31 and Mark 13:27. Secondly, we need to look at the entire picture of the story:

> And one of them, named Caiaphas, being the high priest that same year, said unto them, Ye know nothing at all, Nor consider that it is expedient for us, that one man should die for the people, and that the whole nation perish not. And this spake he not of himself: but being high

> priest that year, he prophesied that Jesus should die for that nation; And not for that nation only, but that also he should gather together in one the children of God that were scattered abroad. John 11:49-52

By the statement *"the children of God that were scattered abroad"*, Caiaphas was still referring to the Jews scattered abroad. He said the nation of Israel would be saved and those Jews who were scattered abroad too. Obviously at that time, the Jews believed that only the Jews would be saved.

In Matthew 24:31 and Mark 13:27, Jesus was referring to the "elect" all over the world; He never said that all Jews are "elect". The fact that someone does not accept Jesus Christ as his or her savior does not mean that Jesus did not die for the person. Jesus died for all.

CALLING

Everything God created has a purpose. They are all for His pleasure. The word "calling", also used as "vocation" in the Bible, describes the purpose of man on earth. Every human being has a calling. Although, we may distinguish Christian calling from others, but everyone has a calling for a specific purpose.

> For the gifts and calling of God are without repentance. Rom. 11:29

According to the scripture, the first calling in the Bible is found in Gen. 12:1:

> By faith Abraham, when he was called to go out into a place which he should after receive for an inheritance, obeyed; and he went out, not knowing whither he went.
> Heb. 11: 8

An "*election*" is a special calling; it could be referred to as a calling into the Faith (see next section). In the New Testament, Peter and Andrew were the first to be called into the fold of Christ.

> Follow me, and I will make you fishers of men.
> Matt. 4:19

All believers have a common calling "to make disciples of all nations". This can be accomplished in different spheres of the society according to our individual gifting. Calling is not limited to preaching or working in the local church. God gives us gifts of talent to excel in whatever purpose He calls us for. Bezaleel was called for a specific art job:

> I have called by name Bezaleel the son of Uri, the son of Hur, of the tribe of Judah: and I have filled him with the spirit of God, in wisdom, and in understanding, and in knowledge, and in all manner of workmanship.
> Exo. 31:2-3

When Paul was called, Jesus said:

> Arise, and go into Damascus; and there it shall be told thee of all things which are appointed for thee to do.
> Acts 22:10

In Paul's exhortation below, he is asking us to be worthy of our calling:

> I therefore, the prisoner of the Lord, beseech you that ye walk worthy of the vocation wherewith ye are called. Eph. 4: 1

ELECTION

The doctrine of election is fiercely debated among Christians because of the various interpretations of the term. The Calvinists posit *unconditional* election while the Arminians say election is *conditional.* Both doctrines speak some truth based on how they view the term "election". There are two types of election: group and individual.

CORPORATE OR GROUP ELECTION

Corporate election is God's choice of a group, the Church, or the nation of Israel, to show that He is the only true God.

> The church that is at Babylon, elected together with you, saluteth you; and so doth Marcus my son. 1Pet 5:13

> For Jacob my servant's sake, and Israel mine elect, I have even called thee by thy name: I have surnamed thee, though thou hast not known me. Isa. 45:4

> The beast of the field shall honour me, the dragons and the owls: because I give waters in the wilderness, and rivers in the desert, to give drink to my people, my chosen. Isa. 43: 20

> Only the LORD had a delight in thy fathers to love them, and he chose their seed after them, even you above all people, as it is this day. Deut. 10:15

Corporate election does not necessarily translate to individual election into Eternal Kingdom as meant in the New Testament.

INDIVIDUAL ELECTION

Individual election is the focus of doctrine of election in the New Testament. It is on this that Calvinists and Arminians have diverse views. There are two groups of people in the scripture that may receive the eternal salvation: they are from the *first* and *second* elections.

First Election

The first elect are those chosen by God for specific purposes in His plan of salvation. Christ is the first elect of the first election; the primary purpose of Jesus' election is to bring people to the knowledge of God and to salvation.

> Behold my servant, whom I uphold; mine elect, in whom my soul delighteth; I have put my spirit upon him: he shall bring forth judgment to the Gentiles. Isa. 42:1

Some angels are part of the first election.

> I charge thee before God, and the Lord Jesus Christ, and the elect angels, that thou observe these things without preferring one before another, doing nothing by partiality. 1Tim 5:21

Some of the first elect men are mentioned in the Old Testament; such people include Abraham (Neh 9:7), Moses (Ps. 106:23) and Jeremiah (Jer. 1:5).

In the New Testament, the word "elect" or "election" is used in 23 verses; 7 in the Gospels by Jesus and 16 in the epistles. In the epistles, the Apostles use the word for both the first and second elections; there is no distinction and that is one of the reasons for the endless debate over the doctrine of election. However, there are two distinct set of men that may receive salvation. We will need to show this through the words of Jesus Christ. In the book of John, Jesus frequently uses "given to me" for the first elect. In regards to men, *first election refers to God's choosing of persons for some type of service towards God's plan of salvation through Jesus Christ.* Let us examine some characteristics of first elect men.

Characteristics of First Elect Men

All first elect men must come to Jesus first:

> All that the Father giveth me shall come to me; and him that cometh to me I will in no wise cast out. John 6: 37

Jesus will protect the first elect:

> My Father, which gave them me, is greater than all; and no man is able to pluck them out of my Father's hand. John 10: 29

The Apostles say the first elect are chosen before the foundation of the world:

According as he hath chosen us in him before the foundation of the world, that we should be holy and without blame before him in love: Eph 1: 4

The Apostles say election is based on foreknowledge:

For whom he did foreknow, he also did predestinate to be conformed to the image of his Son, that he might be the firstborn among many brethren. Rom 8:29

Elect according to the foreknowledge of God the Father, through sanctification of the Spirit, unto obedience and sprinkling of the blood of Jesus Christ: Grace unto you, and peace, be multiplied. 1 Pet 1:2

Apostle Paul says election is not based on foreseen works:

For the children being not yet born, neither having done any good or evil, that the purpose of God according to election might stand, not of works, but of him that calleth; Rom 9:11

First elect must bear fruits that remain:

Ye have not chosen me, but I have chosen you, and ordained you, that ye should go and bring forth fruit, and that your fruit should remain: that whatsoever ye shall ask of the Father in my name, he may give it you.
John 15:16

A first elect man may fall as in the case of Judas:

While I was with them in the world, I kept them in thy name: those that thou gavest me I have kept, and none of them is lost, but the son of perdition; that the scripture might be fulfilled. John 17:12

An elect is just a chosen vessel to be part of God's plan through faith.

> But the Lord said unto him, Go thy way: for he is a chosen vessel unto me, to bear my name before the Gentiles, and kings, and the children of Israel: Acts 9:15

Second Election

In the epistles, the Apostles do not distinguish between the first and the second election. However, Jesus seems to have distinguished the two in the book of John. In John 17:9, Jesus prays for the first elect:

> I pray for them: I pray not for the world, but for them which thou hast given me; for they are thine. John 17:9

He also prays for the other believers that come to Him.

> Neither pray I for these alone, but for them also which shall believe on me through their word; John 17:20

Those who were not "predestinated", but who in the course of life come to Christ and believe on him, belong to this category of election. Perhaps, it is more appropriate not to refer to them as "elect"; however, they are also candidates for the Eternal Kingdom. Simply put, *second election refers to those who were not preordained but who accept Christ as their personal Lord and Savior.* A typical example of a beneficiary of this kind of election was the malefactor crucified on the right hand side of Jesus on Calvary. Note the following passages of scripture:

> Have I any pleasure in the death of the wicked? saith the Lord Jehovah; and not rather that he should return from

his way, and live?... I have no pleasure in the death of him that dieth, saith the Lord Jehovah. Eze. 18:23,32

And it shall come to pass, that whosoever shall call on the name of the Lord shall be saved. Acts 2:21

For whosoever shall call upon the name of the Lord shall be saved. Rom 10:13

And the Spirit and the bride say, Come. And let him that heareth say, Come. And let him that is athirst come. And whosoever will, let him take the water of life freely. Rev. 22:17

Characteristics of Second Election

Second election refers to believers (John 17:20 above)

And this is the will of him that sent me, that every one which seeth the Son, and believeth on him, may have everlasting life: and I will raise him up at the last day. John 6: 40

Second elect men are drawn to Jesus (through universal grace):

No man can come to me, except the Father which hath sent me draw him: and I will raise him up at the last day. John 6: 44

Not all believers are elected:

For many are called, but few are chosen. Matt 22: 14

The possibility of this second chance for election into Eternal Kingdom nullifies the Calvinists' doctrine of reprobation (see Chapter 10).

Common Characteristics of Elections

All elect (first and second) must come to Jesus, see Him, and believe on Him. Jesus promises to protect all.

> All that the Father giveth me shall **come** to me; and him that cometh to me I will in no wise cast out. For I came down from Heaven, not to do mine own will, but the will of him that sent me. And this is the Father's will which hath sent me, that of all which he hath given me I should lose nothing, but should raise it up again at the last day. And this is the will of him that sent me, that every one which **seeth** the Son, and **believeth** on him, may have everlasting life: and I will raise him up at the last day. John 6: 37-40

All elect (first and second) must be faithful.

> These shall make war with the Lamb, and the Lamb shall overcome them: for he is Lord of lords, and King of kings: and they that are with him are called, and chosen, and faithful. Rev 17: 14

Any elect may fall:

> Wherefore the rather, brethren, give diligence to make your calling and election sure: for if ye do these things, ye shall never fall: 2 Pet 1:10

Both first and second elections are through the universal grace and special grace of God; so, the *initial election* itself is *unconditional*. However, since there is a condition that all those who are elected must come to Christ and believe on Him, the validation of election is therefore *conditional*. An initial election remains a potential until validated.

Election to Salvation

Does "chosen" necessarily mean final salvation? The act of salvation only takes placc after birth. Someone can be anointed and chosen for a specific task before birth (first elect):

> Before I formed thee in the belly I knew thee; and before thou camest forth out of the womb I sanctified thee, and I ordained thee a prophet unto the nations. Jer 1: 5

It does not translate to mean everyone is chosen before birth. Not everyone chosen is "God's General". God's Generals have special anointing for specific tasks. Paul says we are chosen to salvation, but not that anyone is saved before birth.

> But we are bound to give thanks alway to God for you, brethren beloved of the Lord, because God hath from the beginning chosen you to salvation through sanctification of the Spirit and belief of the truth: 2 Thess. 2: 13

The process of salvation takes place after birth. We have seen from John 6:37-40 quoted above that no one elect can receive salvation without personally coming to Jesus and believing on Him; this does not take place before birth. Jesus promises to see His sheep through to Eternal Kingdom. His promise here is to win spiritual battles for His sheep (see Security of the Kingdom in Chapter 9). His statements elsewhere indicate that anyone initially elected still needs to worry about personal secondary sins (see Chapter 9) to validate his *final election*. It is doing the Will of God that guarantees Eternal Kingdom.

Not every one that saith unto me, Lord, Lord, shall enter into the Kingdom of Heaven; but he that doeth the will of my Father which is in Heaven. Matt 7:21

8. DOCTRINE OF WORKS

IN *Missional Reformation* (Olowe 2009), the theology of good works is written in detail. In this Chapter, we shall examine the term "works" in general, analyzing the different kinds of works, in order to understand which kind of work is called "*good work*". It is important to understand that works require an interaction with the Society (physical work) or an interaction with God (spiritual work). It is the spiritual work that is relevant in Kingdom justification. So, in this Chapter, we are going to be dealing with the difference between *physical* work and *spiritual* work and the role of each in securing a place in the Kingdom of God. The purpose of good works is to glorify God.

IMPORTANCE OF WORKS

WORK IS GOD ORDAINED

Work, whether physical or spiritual, is ordained of God. At the beginning, God gave man a Will for two purposes, to connect to Him and to manage the earth.

> And the Lord God took the man, and put him into the garden of Eden to dress it and to keep it. Gen 2: 15

> Six days thou shalt labour, and do all thy work:
> Deut. 5:13

After reconnecting to Him, God did not bless Job until he prayed for his friends (Job 42:10). Throughout the scripture, we see the same trend that God's Will for us is to connect to Him and to others through good works, as evident from the Commandments Moses received. It is clear that work is important in the Kingdom. Also, many parables of Jesus are based on stewardship, obedient servants, and business activities.

> How else would the Kingdom of justice and peace come about without human effort? If the sick are to be healed and the hungry fed, does this not imply work on our part? Calvin Redekop and Urie Bender suggest that human work, however necessary, is not an ultimate goal; only God's work and purpose has that distinction. But in the Kingdom to come, our work is fundamentally important to achieve his purpose. It is part of the creation story. (Donald Isaac)

ECONOMIC GROWTH OF NATIONS

> If a man does not work, he gives nothing of value to the world. He is a thief... (Adelaja 2008)

In her book, "*Old Testament Template*", Landa Cope indicates how she saw that though Africa was the most evangelized continent in the world, something had gone wrong and poor countries before the Gospel came had become even poorer. She explains how God revealed to her that "*the devastation you see is the fruit of preaching salvation alone, without the rest of the biblical message.*" She further wrote:

> The message that reformed Western cultures and built nations on solidly Christian values was not the Gospel of salvation, but the Gospel of the Kingdom, which includes salvation. The truths of the Gospel of the Kingdom are to transform us as they teach us how to live every part of life. Our transformed lives are then to be salt and light to our families, neighbourhoods, communities and finally, our nations, making them better places to live for everyone. Not perfect communities, not Heaven on earth, but better because the influence of good is as great, if not greater, than evil. There have been great examples of this in history.

The rest of the biblical message Landa is talking about here is "good works". Similarly in her book, Barbara Ward suggests that one of the four primary ideas in the history of civilization responsible for wealth is stewardship. Good work as we shall see is both physical and spiritual.

PURPOSEFUL LIFE

Life without a purpose is meaningless (Warren) and work gives a man a reason for living. We gain confidence, self-respect, dignity, and self-worth through our work. A man should work to the best of his ability and enjoy the fruits of such activity (Tucker).

> Whatsoever thy hand findeth to do, do it with thy might; for there is no work, nor device, nor knowledge, nor wisdom, in the grave, whither thou goest. Eccl 9: 10

> Behold that which I have seen: it is good and comely for one to eat and to drink, and to enjoy the good of all his labour that he taketh under the sun all the days of his life, which God giveth him: for it is his portion. Eccl 5: 18

PHYSICAL WORKS

Physical works connect us to other men. In the Old Testament, there are 613 laws or so given to the nation of Israel which theologians usually distribute over three categories: civic (or civil), ceremonial, and moral laws. Theologians also assert that the moral laws are the only ones relevant to the Church. The civil laws are relevant to the Society and the ceremonial laws are relevant to specific cultures. The moral laws are what form the basis of Kingdom principles. In the same analogy, Work can be categorized into three: *civic*, *ceremonial*, and *moral* (or Kingdom) work. Civic and Kingdom works are very important to man. Civic work is relevant to the Society while moral work is relevant to the Kingdom of God. Let us briefly look at the importance of these three categories of physical works.

CIVIC WORKS

A civic work is very important for every living person. Here are some of the reasons why a man does civic work.

1. Civic work is what a man does to earn a living. It is through this work that man is able to provide for his family and needs.

> But if any provide not for his own, and specially for those of his own house, he hath denied the faith, and is worse than an infidel. 1 Tim 5: 8

2: There are some people who cannot work, perhaps due to some disabilities or for other reasons. God says there will always be poor people among you.

> For the poor shall never cease out of the land: therefore I command thee, saying, Thou shalt open thine hand wide unto thy brother, to thy poor, and to thy needy, in thy land. Deut. 15:11

Civic work gives a man the ability to help those who are less fortunate.

> Let him that stole steal no more: but rather let him labour, working with his hands the thing which is good, that he may have to give to him that needeth. Eph 4: 28

In other words, a man needs civic work to effectuate good works. Good works will be discussed under Moral or Kingdom works and also under Spiritual Works.

3. Civic work enables a man to contribute to the economy and development of his community through payment of taxes and donations. Jesus Christ paid taxes.

> And he said unto them, Render therefore unto Caesar the things which be Caesar's, and unto God the things which be God's. Luke 20:25, Mark 12:17, Matt 22:21

4. Civic work enables a man to develop skills that may be needed for Kingdom work. To build the temple, Solomon looked for people who had regular jobs and who can use their skills for the work of God.

> Send me now therefore a man cunning to work in gold, and in silver, and in brass, and in iron, and in purple, and crimson, and blue, and that can skill to grave with the cunning men that are with me in Judah and in Jerusalem, whom David my father did provide. 2Chr 2:7

Talents are gifts from God, but skills are developed. Over the years, I have developed skills in teaching, graphics, computer programming, and research; they are all proving useful for my calling.

CEREMONIAL WORKS

Ceremonial works are works that we do to make things look right before men or before God; they are mostly specific to a culture. Ceremonial works are complex; since they could involve God or men, they could be physical or spiritual. Ceremonial works include events, hospitality, festivals, rituals, anniversaries, fasting, and all kinds of physical and religious ceremonies. Usually, people do not earn a living from ceremonial works. In the Old Testament, those works include sacrifices, observing Passover, circumcision, and so on. These are the works Apostle Paul calls "*works of the law*", as discussed in Chapter 1. When a ceremonial work is intended to make things right before God (such as *works of the law*), it is work done to maintain connection to God (salvation).

On a positive side, some ceremonial works can add values in the Kingdom. When someone works in a Church ministry, such as in the choir or volunteers to do something in the Church (see difference between a Church ministry and a Missional ministry in *Missional Reformation* (Olowe 2009)), he or she is working with God's people and not with ungodly people. Even though those works are ceremonial works and not Kingdom works, but they are essential because some people have to do them. They help to "service" one's salvation. They are "*good ceremonial works*".

Some good ceremonial works could be distracting. The story of Mary and her sister Martha, when Jesus visited them, illustrates how ceremonial work could be distracting.

> And Jesus answered and said unto her, Martha, Martha, thou art careful and troubled about many things: But one thing is needful: and Mary hath chosen that good part, which shall not be taken away from her. Luke 10: 41-42

Also, the scripture emphasizes that obedience (as in Kingdom work) is better than ceremonial work in some cases.

> And Samuel said, Hath the Lord as great delight in burnt offerings and sacrifices, as in obeying the voice of the Lord? Behold, to obey is better than sacrifice, and to hearken than the fat of rams. 1 Sam 15: 22

Some ceremonial works are good and acceptable to the Lord but some could also be evil. As a matter of fact, ceremonial works not based on Christian principles can lead to occultism and as such are *evil ceremonial works.*

MORAL (KINGDOM) WORKS

Moral works are both physical and spiritual, that is, they involve other men and God. As revealed in "*Missional Reformation*" (Olowe 2009), and discussed under "The Kingdom of God" below, the Gospel of works is derived from the second Great Commandment: "*thou shalt love thy neighbour as thyself*" which is an abridged form of the last six of the Ten Commandments. Moral (or Kingdom) works are works that show love and compassion towards other people as illustrated by the parable of the Good Samaritan (Luke 10:30-37). The "neighbour" in the second Great Commandment refers to the Gentiles in the books of law. A moral work should therefore rather connect to the unbelievers than our church members. A moral work must reach out to the society. Works that only reach out to church members or other Christians are defined above as ceremonial works. A moral or

Kingdom work is therefore what is known as *good work.* The five cardinal principles of good works (Olowe 2009) are:

1. making disciples (evangelizing) (Matt 28:19);
2. making peace (Heb 12:14);
3. giving (Luke 11:41);
4. stewardship (Gen. 2:15, Matt 21:43);
5. enlightening of the world (Matt 5:14-16, Rom 12:2);

Two of the cardinal principles of good works (discipling and enlightening) require one to be saved first. One's good work after salvation is therefore better than before salvation.

> Forasmuch as ye are manifestly declared to be the epistle of Christ ministered by us, written not with ink, but with the Spirit of the living God; not in tables of stone, but in fleshy tables of the heart. 2 Cor. 3: 3

The tables of stone here are the Gospel of God which includes good works and salvation. God lives only in the heart of the regenerate. To effectuate good work, it is better to have the Holy Spirit residing in the heart first.

What John Wesley termed as *Works of Mercy (*Doing Good, Giving, Visitations, Feeding and Clothing those in need, and so on) as the second part of the *Means of Grace* is simply good works.

A civic work could be counted as a Kingdom work in a situation where the work implements one of the cardinal principles of good works highlighted above. Typical examples are the full time Pastoral or Evangelical works.

SPIRITUAL WORKS

While a physical work may not involve God, a spiritual work connects to both other men and to God. Spiritual works are the ones that justify a man of works before God to gain access into his Kingdom. Biblically, the opposite of good is evil. With this, one can define three kinds of spiritual works: *good*, *evil*, and *no* works. All the three are mentioned in the scripture.

EVIL WORKS

Evil work is mentioned in several verses in the scripture.

> Yea, better is he than both they, which hath not yet been, who hath not seen the evil work that is done under the sun. Eccl 4: 3
>
> Because sentence against an evil work is not executed speedily, therefore the heart of the sons of men is fully set in them to do evil. Eccl 8: 11
>
> Beware of dogs, beware of evil workers, beware of the concision. Philip 3: 2
>
> And the Lord shall deliver me from every evil work, and will preserve me unto his Heavenly Kingdom: to whom be glory for ever and ever. Amen. 2 Tim 4: 18
>
> For where envying and strife is, there is confusion and every evil work. James 3: 16

An *evil work* (negative spiritual work) results from violating the second Great Commandment, that is, those Commandments of God that relates us to others. Violations include murder, stealing, adultery, covetousness, and so on. Evil works lead to sin. The scripture clearly stipulates that *evil works* will certainly exclude one from the Kingdom of God.

> For this ye know, that no whoremonger, nor unclean person, nor covetous man, who is an idolater, hath any inheritance in the Kingdom of Christ and of God.
> Eph. 5:5

> Whosoever hateth his brother is a murderer: and ye know that no murderer hath eternal life abiding in him.
> 1 John 3: 15

Sin is not committed from what goes from the body into the soul, like what you see or what you hear or what you eat or what you touch innocently; but the moment information is processed negatively in the soul, sin is committed already even before it is communicated back to the body (see Chapter 4 under "Illustration of Man").

> Not that which goeth into the mouth defileth a man; but that which cometh out of the mouth, this defileth a man.
> Matt 15:11

> For out of the heart proceed evil thoughts, murders, adulteries, fornications, thefts, false witness, blasphemies:
> Matt. 15:19

> But I say unto you, That whosoever looketh on a woman to lust after her hath committed adultery with her already in his heart. Matt. 5: 28

GOOD WORKS

A *good work* (positive spiritual work) has been defined as a Kingdom work. It involves the obedience of the second Great Commandment to love one another. A good work is not only just obeying the Commandments of God relating to human relationships, it puts faith into action in order to improve the moral values of the society towards a Christ-like end. In order to implement good works, one needs to utilize God's universal and special grace to serve and profit others.

> Seek not every man his own things, but every man the good of his brothers. I Cor. 10:24.

The purpose of good works is to please and glorify God.

Benefits of good works

Reward in the Kingdom is in proportion of Good Works

> For the Son of man shall come in the glory of his Father with his angels; and then he shall reward every man according to his works. Matt. 16: 27

> Rejoice, and be exceeding glad: for great is your reward in Heaven: for so persecuted they the prophets which were before you. (Matt. 5: 12; Luke 6:23, 35)

> Knowing that of the Lord ye shall receive the reward of the inheritance: for ye serve the Lord Christ. But he that doeth wrong shall receive for the wrong which he hath done: and there is no respect of persons. Col 3: 24-25

> And, behold, I come quickly; and my reward is with me, to give every man according as his work shall be. Rev 22: 12

Implementation of Good Works

In *Missional Reformation* (Olowe 2009), *Churchshift* is described as currently one of the best models to implement good works. Churchshift is not a program to be implemented by a church as a corporate body. It is a program developed by individual members of a church to reach out to the society. In Churchshift, believers disciple in their areas of gifting. Churchshift is defined as "*discipling nations by stewardship*". Discipling covers all spheres of the society.

NO WORKS

A *no works* (neutral spiritual work) situation occurs when neither the second Great Commandment is violated nor is there any active good work. For a saved person, this is the position of a *passive* believer, with a "dead faith" according to James.

> Even so faith, if it hath no works, is dead, being alone.
> James 2:17

Can a believer with no works make the Eternal Kingdom? Yes, but under a certain condition. A perfect example to demonstrate this is the malefactor crucified with Jesus on the right hand side (Luke 23:39-43). He accepted Jesus Christ as his Lord and Savior, and hence he immediately received salvation. His past sins and those he inherited from Adam were wiped off. Our good work is one of the things God can use to justify us of our personal sins after receiving salvation (see Chapter 9). At the moment of death, there was no personal sin to be brought for judgment, so the malefactor was justified by salvation and of his works. The only thing, though, is that he has no reward to claim because of zero work. However, his could be an exceptional case in Heaven. Besides, the preaching to the other malefactor could have been counted for him as good works.

Since man is not able not to sin, the only condition for a man to enter into the Kingdom of God with no works is to accept Jesus at his point of death. It is clear that a person with no works, even if he/she makes the Kingdom of God, has no reward there. He/she will be the least there.

THE KINGDOM OF GOD

This Section recaps the revelations about the Kingdom of God that has been published in "*Missional Reformation*" (Olowe 2009). The current project actually started with two revelations, one from the scripture and the other from a vision. The essence of the revelations is to understand the requirements for the Kingdom of God. The two revelations have also been discussed in *Missional Reformation* book. It is essential to also discuss them here so that we know the origin of the current research work.

SCRIPTURAL REVELATION

First, it was revealed by the Holy Spirit that the Gospel of God is two Gospels in one which are derived from the Great Commandments. In the Old Testament, Moses received from God the Ten Commandments in two slabs of stone. These Commandments are the Gospel of God. God purposely gave them in two slabs, both times they were written. Also, Jesus cited two passages (Deut. 6:5 and Lev. 19:18) where all the laws have been summarized into two Great Commandments. The two Great Commandments, which represent the Gospel of God, are illustrated in Figure 8.1.

Figure 8.1: The Great Commandments (Gospel of God)

The texts of the two Great Commandments are:

> Thou shalt love the Lord thy God with all thy heart, and with all thy soul, and with all thy mind. Matt 22:37

> Thou shalt love thy neighbour as thyself. Matt 22:39

Jesus says that all laws and prophets hang on these two Great Commandments.

We can notice that the two Great Commandments are not drawn out from the same book (one in Deuteronomy and the other in Leviticus); Jesus fished them out. The two indications are not coincidental; God's two slabs and Jesus' two Great Commandments. God and Jesus know that God purposely separates laws that deal with Him from laws that deal with men. The two slabs of stone represent the Gospel of God in two parts. We so much stress it in this book that the Will of God for mankind is basically to have good relationship with Him and for men to have good relationship with each other. He intentionally separated the two Gospels when He gave the laws to Moses and Jesus recognized that.

PICTORIAL REVELATION

The second revelation is pictorial as illustrated in Figure 8.2. I saw the three pictures of Figure 8.2 in a vision. The pictures show that neither salvation alone nor good works alone can lead to the Kingdom of God; this was also the inference from the scriptural revelation.

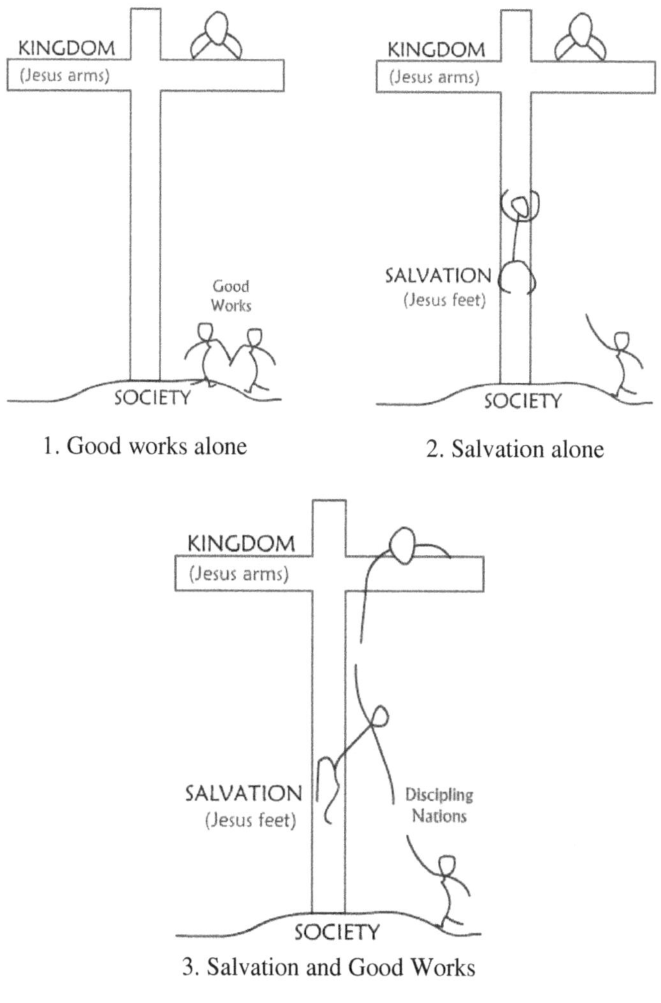

Figure 8.2: Reaching the Kingdom of God

The first image of Figure 8.2 shows clearly the situation of good works alone. The man at the "Kingdom" stayed indifferent and was looking at the two people.

The second image, although interpreted as "salvation alone" could more aptly be interpreted as "salvation with *evil works"* because the one who received salvation intentionally refused to help the other. Evil work is defined above.

The third image shows the perfect scenario to gain access to the Kingdom of God.

FULL GOSPEL

It is worth noting that loving God leads us to salvation, and loving others leads us to good works. Somehow, both are intertwined because we cannot claim to love God if we don't love our neighbour (1 John 4:20) and also, to see God, one needs to be holy and have peace with all men (Heb 12:14).

A Full Gospel Church is a church that teaches and practices both the Gospel of salvation and the Gospel of good works. The Gospel of the Kingdom of God is in two parts.

Kingdom = Salvation + Good Works

A Missional Church must be a Full Gospel Church.

9. JUSTIFICATION

JUSTIFICATION is commonly defined as the judicial act of God by which He declares or makes a sinner righteous before Him. Justification removes the guilt and penalty of sin as if they never happened. The opposite of justification is condemnation. Bible Encyclopedia (christian-answers.net) explains further:

> In addition to the pardon of sin, justification declares that all the claims of the law are satisfied in respect of the justified. It is the act of a judge and not of a sovereign. The law is not relaxed or set aside, but is declared to be fulfilled in the strictest sense; and so the person justified is declared to be entitled to all the advantages and rewards arising from perfect obedience to the law (Rom. 5:1-10)

Declaring a man righteous before God is the actual usage of justification in the Old Testament and by the Lord Jesus during His ministry. It should be the correct usage. Making us right with God implies that we are in line with His Will which is always twofold: being right with Him and being right with one another. The second part, "making it right with one another", has been systematically removed from Church doctrine from the early Church, and James' emphasis on it has been conveniently ignored.

ORIGIN OF THE TERM

The term "justification" originates from God Himself in the Old Testament. Jesus Christ used it in the Gospel and only Paul and James used the term in the epistles. Before we enter into the discussion of Paul and James' justification theology, it is better to examine first the word from the Lord. What does God say through the prophets about justification? How did Jesus use the term?

USE OF THE TERM IN THE OLD TESTAMENT

The term relating to justification before God is found in 23 verses of the Old Testament (OT). Let us analyze some of these passages. The general theme in the OT is that only the righteous will be justified and that righteousness is not only with God but also in our relationships with each other. There are hundreds of passages forbidding wickedness (opposite of righteousness in the Bible) to one another. In the OT, God is really serious about our relationships with each other and promulgated several laws on this.

> Thou shalt not raise a false report: put not thine hand with the wicked to be an unrighteous witness. Exo. 23: 1. Keep thee far from a false matter; and the innocent and righteous slay thou not: for I will not justify the wicked. Exo. 23: 7
>
> If there be a controversy between men, and they come unto judgment, that the judges may judge them; then they shall justify the righteous, and condemn the wicked. Deut. 25: 1
>
> Then hear thou in Heaven, and do, and judge thy servants, condemning the wicked, to bring his way upon his head; and justifying the righteous, to give him according to his righteousness. I Kings 8: 32; 2 Chr. 6: 23

Although Jesus' propitiation covers us for our sins before salvation, we are still liable to being good to our neighbours and environment.

USE OF THE TERM BY JESUS

Jesus used the term on four occasions and in three of those occasions, it was to rebuke the Pharisees.

1. When Jesus preached that John the Baptist was His forerunner; people who had repented and baptized by John praised God for being justified. In contrast, the Pharisees and lawyers rejected in the counsel of God believing in their own way of justification, Jesus rebuked them:

> For John the Baptist came neither eating bread nor drinking wine; and ye say, He hath a devil. The Son of man came eating and drinking, and they say, Behold a man gluttonous, and a winebibber, a friend of publicans and sinners. But wisdom is justified of her children. Matt. 11: 18; Luke 7: 33-35

Application Bible's comments:

> Jesus condemned the attitude of his generation. No matter what he said or did, they took the opposite view. They were cynical and skeptical because he challenged their comfortable, secure, and self-centered lives. Too often we justify our inconsistencies because listening to God may require us to change the way we live.
>
> The Pharisees weren't troubled by their inconsistency toward John the Baptist and Jesus. They were good at justifying their "wisdom".

So, the use of justification here by Jesus is in respect of not counting on our wisdom but on the Will of God, including our relationship with each other.

2. On the second occasion in the passage below, Jesus was accused by the religious leaders of using satan to cast out demons. He told them that it is a blasphemy to the Holy Ghost and it is a sin.

> But I say unto you, That every idle word that men shall speak, they shall give account thereof in the day of judgment. For by thy words thou shalt be justified, and by thy words thou shalt be condemned. Matt. 12: 36-37

3. On the third occasion, it was a parable of two men who prayed; one is self righteous and despises the other.

> I tell you, this man went down to his house justified rather than the other: for every one that exalteth himself shall be abased; and he that humbleth himself shall be exalted. Luke 18: 14

The parable is about who is doing God's Will. God detest the proud heart.

4. On the fourth occasion, after the parable of the shrewd accountant, the covetous Pharisees derided Jesus:

> And he said unto them, Ye are they which justify yourselves before men; but God knoweth your hearts: for that which is highly esteemed among men is abomination in the sight of God. The law and the prophets were until John: since that time the Kingdom of God is preached, and every man presseth into it. And it is easier for Heaven and earth to pass, than one little of the law to fail. Luke 16: 15-17

Here again we see that Jesus is talking about the Kingdom of God. So, justification is for gaining entrance into the Kingdom of God. There are other occasions in which the term "justification" is not directly used but in which Jesus is talking about it; from His statement one can imply that he is talking about the importance of one's *spiritual works* to qualify for eternal Kingdom of God. Here is an example:

> Marvel not at this: for the hour is coming, in the which all that are in the graves shall hear his voice, And shall

> come forth; they that have done good, unto the resurrection of life; and they that have done evil, unto the resurrection of damnation. John 5: 28-29

UNDERSTANDING JUSTIFICATION

The biblical use of the word justification indicates that we are justified when we are right with God's Will to have good relationship with Him and with our neighbours and God pronounces us of not guilty of any sin. Application Study Bible also defines Justification as *God's act of declaring us "not guilty" for our sins*. It is true, but which sins are covered in justification? Certainly, Jesus' blood justifies man for sins before salvation (Adam's and personal). But is the propitiation of Jesus enough to cover our wickedness towards ourselves after gaining salvation? In order words, if you go and murder someone after gaining salvation, extra steps are needed to cover those sins. So, there are two different set of sins to be justified of:

1. *Primary sins*: Adam's transmitted sin and one's personal sins before initial salvation;
2. *Secondary sins*: One's personal sins (evil works) after gaining salvation.

Here, we see again the pattern of pairs that is so frequent in this book. Justification for the Kingdom of God must cover the two Great Commandments and it is in two parts: *justification of primary sins by salvation* and *justification of sec-*

ondary sins by works. Justification is not either by faith or by works; one has to be justified by both. In Galatians 6:7-10 Paul writes:

> Be not deceived; God is not mocked: for whatsoever a man soweth, that shall he also reap. For he that soweth to his flesh shall of the flesh reap corruption; but he that soweth to the Spirit shall of the Spirit reap life everlasting. And let us not be weary in well doing: for in due season we shall reap, if we faint not. As we have therefore opportunity, let us do good unto all men, especially unto them who are of the household of faith. Gal. 6: 7-10

We see that Paul is also saying it here; "life everlasting" is the Kingdom of God. Your works matter to enter into the Kingdom of God.

JUSTIFICATION BY SALVATION

Salvation justifies man of the *primary sins* defined above. Paul is the chief proponent of justification by salvation. When he preached to the Jews in Antioch of Pisidia, he said:

> And by him all that believe are justified from all things, from which ye could not be justified by the law of Moses. Acts 13: 39

And in his letter to the Galatians, he says:

> No man is justified by the law in the sight of God, it is evident: for, The just shall live by faith. Gal. 3: 11

This is what Luther and the 16th century reformers picked up. Paul has not contradicted Jesus' usage of justification, but he has just provided a partial justification of entrance into the Kingdom of God. Paul is saying that we are justified by the blotting out of our sin by Jesus and we do not need to perfectly obey the law because "by the law is the knowledge of sin" (Rom. 3:20). Paul says in Romans 3:24 that we are justified by the redemption in Christ Jesus. Paul's message is directed at those who are yet to accept the Faith, the non-believers. They need salvation first before they can understand the importance of good works. Paul's messages can be understood that we are justified by doing God's Will rather than perfectly obeying the law. Fine, but salvation is just part of God's Will (discussed in *Missional Reformation*" (Olowe 2009)). The other part deals with relationships with each other (works). By the way, let us examine another usage by Paul in his epistle to the Romans. He says:

> (For not the hearers of the law are just before God, but the doers of the law shall be justified. Rom. 2: 13

He is talking about the moral laws here which are not only about salvation, but also about good works. So, Paul has not contradicted the intended usage, but he just narrowed his thought to salvation, perhaps because of his zeal after being converted and the focus then to establish Christianity. In another passage Paul writes:

> God forbid: yea, let God be true, but every man a liar; as it is written, THAT THOU MIGHTEST BE JUSTIFIED IN

> THY SAYINGS, AND MIGHTEST OVERCOME WHEN THOU ART JUDGED. Rom. 3: 4

The scripture Paul is quoting here is from Psalm 51:4 that David wrote after violating God's second Great Commandment of "*Thou shall love thy neighbour as thy self*", from which the Gospel of good works is derived. We see that justification in the last two mentioned passages includes good works. Paul uses the term "justification" or "justified" in 22 verses and his focus is on salvation by Christ Jesus. Paul's justification is "Justification of Salvation". It takes care of Adam's sin and all our sins before salvation.

JUSTIFICATION OF WORKS

We see in Chapter 8 that there are three kinds of *spiritual works:* evil, good, and no works. Evil works lead to sins. Every of man's spiritual work is brought before God for judgment:

> For God shall bring every work into judgment, with every secret thing, whether it be good, or whether it be evil. Eccl 12: 14

Good works can justify man of *secondary sins* defined above; we can appropriately call it *justification of works by good works*. James provides arguments for justification by works and this does not go well with Reformed theologians. James was the brother of Jesus who led the early Christians with Peter. In three verses, James writes:

> Was not Abraham our father justified by works, when he had offered Isaac his son upon the altar? James 2: 21

> Ye see then how that by works a man is justified, and not by faith only. James 2: 24

> Likewise also was not Rahab the harlot justified by works, when she had received the messengers, and had sent them out another way? James 2: 25

The first and third passages show obedience to the Will of God, one through Abraham's connection to Him (first Great Commandment – faith or salvation) and the other through Rahab's help of the Israelites (second Great Commandment – good works). The second passage is a declaration. We see here that James shows the two purposes of God's creation (good relationship with Him and with others), His Will. So, James understood the concept of justification better than Paul. If the book of James had been missing from the Bible, we would probably not be having the prolonged debate. But then, God is wonderful. Some Calvinists have tried to put a spin on James writings but the statements are too straight forward, difficult to spin; so, they prefer ignoring it and use only Paul's writings as God's word. On newadvent.org, the Catholics make the following statements:

> Martin Luther stands as the originator of the doctrine of justification by faith alone... Luther rejected the Epistle of St. James as "one of straw" and into the text of St. Paul to the Romans (3:28) he boldly inserted the word "alone". This falsification of the Bible was certainly not done in the spirit of the Apostle's teaching, for nowhere does St. Paul teach that faith alone (without charity) will bring

> justification, even though we should accept as also Pauline the text given in a different context, that supernatural faith alone justifies but the fruitless works of the Jewish Law do not. (newadvent.org/cathen/06701a.htm)

In 1 Corinthians 6:9-11, Paul assures believers that they are justified because their *primary* sins are washed away by the blood of Jesus. He does not speak of the believers' *secondary* sins after salvation.

> Know ye not that the unrighteous shall not inherit the Kingdom of God? Be not deceived: neither fornicators, nor idolaters, nor adulterers, nor effeminate, nor abusers of themselves with mankind, nor thieves, nor covetous, nor drunkards, nor revilers, nor extortioners, shall inherit the Kingdom of God. And such were some of you: but ye are washed, but ye are sanctified, but ye are justified in the name of the Lord Jesus, and by the Spirit of our God.
> I Cor 6: 9-11

However, in another passage, Paul warns the saints against unrighteousness:

> But fornication, and all uncleanness, or covetousness, let it not be once named among you, as becometh saints;
> Eph 5: 3

The two passages above suggest that Paul agrees with justification of works at the Kingdom gate irrespective of gaining salvation or not. Also in Ephesians 2:10,

> For we are His workmanship, created in Christ Jesus for good works, which God prepared beforehand that we should walk in them. Eph 2:10

Paul is saying here that God's intention is that our salvation will result in good works which would account for our justification. In Romans 2:13, Paul also agrees with justification by works.

> (For not the hearers of the law are just before God, but the doers of the law shall be justified. Rom 2: 13

SECURITY OF THE KINGDOM

Calvinism uses the term "perseverance of the saints" instead of "security of the Kingdom." We have seen that man needs to be justified of the primary and secondary sins by salvation and by works respectively. Let us examine the security in each of these cases. We recall that Jesus says:

> Not every one that saith unto me, Lord, Lord, shall enter into the Kingdom of Heaven; but he that doeth the will of my Father which is in Heaven. Matt. 7: 21

As we have discussed in Chapters 4 and 5, the Will of God for man is salvation and good works. So a believer needs to secure a place in the Kingdom of God on two grounds. This can be understood through the illustration revealed to me.

Figure 9.1, a revelation, shows an illustration of the path taken by the believer to reach the Kingdom of God. The illustration shows three stages that a believer must go through in order to reach the Eternal Kingdom. The stages include a Christian salvation life in between two gates.

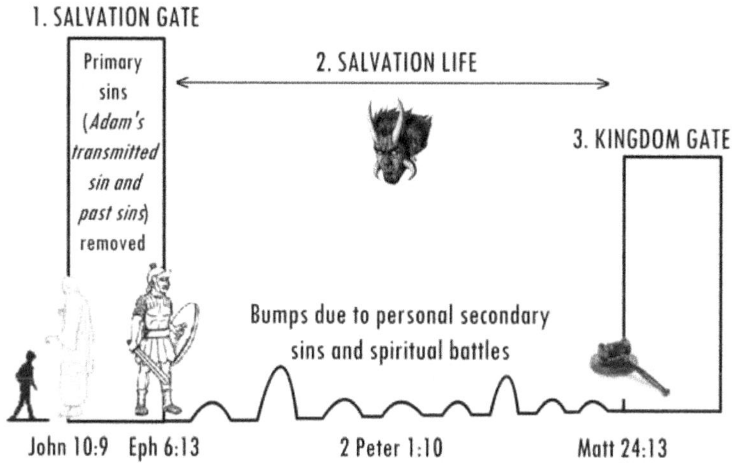

Figure 9.1: Path to the Kingdom of God

STAGE 1: SALVATION GATE

At the first gate, a believer receives the *Initial Salvation* through Jesus Christ. This is the most important stage in human life. No amount of human efforts can guarantee entrance into salvation life. It is only by the grace of God.

> I am the door: by me if any man enter in, he shall be saved, and shall go in and out, and find pasture. Joh 10:9

At this gate, Jesus Christ takes away the *primary sins* (Adam's transmitted sin and the past personal sins) of the believer up to that moment.

> Whom God hath set forth to be a propitiation through faith in his blood, to declare his righteousness for the re-

> mission of sins that are past, through the forbearance of God; Rom 3: 25

This stage is the most crucial because one needs salvation first to be able to connect to God (see Chapter 4) before even thinking of the Kingdom of God. It is crucial because satan also erects multiple gates to deceive people; Jesus used "gates" in the plural in Matt 16:18 for hell. To find the right gate is by God's grace (Matt 7:14).

> Neither is there salvation in any other: for there is none other name under Heaven given among men, whereby we must be saved. Acts 4: 12

If we go through the scriptures, we find that there are gates in the physical realm and in the spiritual realm. In both cases, they are usually the stronghold of the community and there battles are fought (see Isa. 28:6 for example). Apostle Paul advises that the believer takes up the armor of God at this gate because he or she will go through spiritual battles.

> Wherefore take unto you the whole armour of God, that ye may be able to withstand in the evil day, and having done all, to stand. Eph 6: 13

Salvation in Christ Jesus covers the *primary* sins of the believer. Unless the believer apostatizes (that is, defects) in the Salvation Life stage, once saved, a person is no longer liable for the original and previous sins; he did nothing to earn his salvation. But after gaining access to salvation, the believer needs works and faith to secure a place in Heaven.

STAGE 2: SALVATION LIFE

The Salvation Life stage is critical because it is this stage that determines if a man will be justified before God; it is at this stage one can fall from grace.

> Wherefore let him that thinketh he standeth take heed lest he fall. 1 Cor 10: 12

All those who enter this second stage form the Body of Christ (the Church). The Salvation Life stage can also be called the Kingdom of God on Earth. Right from the Salvation Gate, satan is there waiting for the believer. Spiritual battles are expected at this stage to prevent the believer from getting to the end.

> And many false prophets shall rise, and shall deceive many. And because iniquity shall abound, the love of many shall wax cold. Matt 24: 11-12

Besides satan's deceptions, one's secondary sins also come as obstacles to advance towards the Kingdom Gate. Therefore *spiritual battles* and *secondary sins*, represented by the bumps and small hills within the Salvation Life stage of Figure 9.1, are the two obstacles the believer faces. The stage requires both the grace of God and human efforts. The span of the stage is time dependent. If the time span of the stage is zero, then the believer can go from the salvation gate straight to the Kingdom gate; this is the case of the malefactor crucified on the right hand side of Jesus. Let us examine how to overcome the bumps from the two major obstacles.

Spiritual Battles

If a believer apostatizes (that is, defects), it is because he/she has lost a spiritual battle to satan. In order to overcome and win spiritual battles, the believer needs to do the following:

1. Pray and fast regularly.

> Praying always with all prayer and supplication in the Spirit, and watching thereunto with all perseverance and supplication for all saints; Eph 6: 18

> Defraud ye not one the other, except it be with consent for a time, that ye may give yourselves to fasting and prayer; and come together again, that satan tempt you not for your incontinency. I Cor 7: 5

2. Resist counterfeit knowledge from satan. Don't be led away by false doctrine. This is important.

> ...beware lest ye also, being led away with the error of the wicked, fall from your own steadfastness. 2 Pet. 3:17

3. Be steadfast, that is, continue in His goodness. A believer must persevere in the faith.

> Behold therefore the goodness and severity of God: on them which fell, severity; but toward thee, goodness, if thou continue in His goodness: otherwise thou also shalt be cut off. Rom. 11:22

Personal Secondary Sins

The personal sins within the Salvation Life stage are labeled "*secondary*" to distinguish them from the *primary* sins (that is the sins that one carries to the Salvation Gate). Basically, personal secondary sins are what a Christian needs to worry about. All mankind will be justified of your *spiritual works*, elect or no elect; it is also confirmed from John 5:29 and Galatians 6:7-10 quoted previously. This makes the Calvinists doctrine of predestination strange and irrational. It will be discussed in Chapter 10. The doctrine gives a false sense of security to the believer; it implies that once an unregenerate goes to church to recite some statements of accepting Jesus, he is forever saved, and for sure, Heaven is guaranteed. False! If justification of works does not exist, man will be doing one evil after another as it pleases him, even after gaining salvation. So, how can secondary sins in the Salvation Life stage be relaxed by God towards being pronounced "not guilty" and to secure a place in Heaven? If a believer is able to go through the entire span of the Salvation Life stage, he/she is already justified of works. We know that once you are saved, you are no longer under the law.

> For sin shall not have dominion over you: for ye are not under the law, but under grace. Romans 6: 14

However, the following two must be accomplished in order to have the secondary sins relaxed and be in good standing with God's Will:

1. Repentance - Prayer of Forgiveness

> If my people, which are called by my name, shall humble themselves, and pray, and seek my face, and turn from their wicked ways; then will I hear from Heaven, and will forgive their sin, and will heal their land. 2 Chr. 7:14

Jesus preached severally on forgiveness, He even included it in the Lord's Prayer on purpose. A Christian needs to understand the doctrine of forgiveness. Because man is not able not to sin, one should pray everyday for forgiveness or thank God for forgiveness. One of the ordinances of forgiveness is to forgive others.

> For if ye forgive men their trespasses, your Heavenly Father will also forgive you: Matt 6:14

2. Good works

> Wherefore the rather, brethren, give diligence to make your calling and election sure: for if ye do these things, ye shall never fall: 2 Pet. 1: 10

I discussed with a preacher who claims that he does not need good works to reach the Kingdom of God if he obeys the Commandments and he is steadfast in the faith till the end. True, but the Commandments include being good to the needy. The Catholics also say almost the same thing, that Kingdom can be attained through "*salutary acts or a state of holiness*"; that is, through good works or holiness. As discussed in Chapter 8, a holy passive believer with *no works* may also reach the Kingdom, but he/she would not have any reward to claim there. Anyway, it is safe to follow Paul's advice: *let him that thinketh he standeth take heed lest he fall* (1 Cor 10:12). No one, who lives after receiving salvation, can avoid good works to reach the Kingdom. The fact that *evil works* (sins) create obstacles to advance to the Kingdom

Gate automatically implies that one is justified of works if one is able to reach the Kingdom Gate.

Your good works, especially almsgiving and helping others, could be a replacement for sacrifice as relaxation of personal secondary sins and redemption from calamity as in the Old Testament. Almsgiving is an act of helping the poor and needy; it is an expression of compassion, empathy, and love for the poor and needy. If you have empathy for others, you will get it in return from God. Almsgiving is also counted for us as righteousness.

> But rather give alms of such things as ye have; and, behold, all things are clean unto you. Luke 11:41

"Clean unto you" means righteousness. Righteousness can relax God's wrath, not the riches one keeps:

> Riches profit not in the day of wrath: but righteousness delivereth from death. Prov. 11:4

> By mercy and truth iniquity is purged: and by the fear of the Lord men depart from evil. Prov. 16: 6

> To do justice and judgment is more acceptable to the Lord than sacrifice. Prov. 21:3

It is important to state that God's forgiveness of a believer's secondary sins by praying for forgiveness and by good works as presented above is possible because of the believer's connection to Jesus and the Holy Spirit that resides in the heart. Jesus' blood is not ordinary. A believer needs to consider the two points above (repentance and good works) in order to remove the obstacles from sins (evil works) on the path of advancing to the Kingdom gate. Paul actually mentioned the two conditions in a statement to Agrippa: *"that they should repent and turn to God, and do works meet for repentance"* (Acts 26:20b). This is how a believer is justified of works; that is, he is pronounced not guilty of secondary sins.

STAGE 3: THE KINGDOM GATE

The gate of the Eternal Kingdom of God follows the Salvation Life stage (Kingdom on Earth).

> But he that shall endure unto the end, the same shall be saved. Matt 24:13

Reaching the Kingdom gate is what Jesus calls "the end". This "*Final Salvation*" is therefore the Eternal Kingdom of God. Once a believer is able to reach the Kingdom Gate, he should have been justified of both primary and secondary sins by salvation and works respectively. The good news is that, Jesus promises to take the believer to the end (John 6:37-40) by taking care of spiritual battles if he perseveres (Matt 24:13) and does the Will of God (Matt 7:21). All those given to Christ by God are those who God draws to Him (John 6:44) through the universal grace to receive the special grace. The Father's Will is that not one of those who were given to the Son should be rejected or lost by him.

10. PROBLEMS WITH CALVINISM

THE two generally adopted doctrines of grace found in protestant churches today are Calvinism and Arminianism (Classical and Wesleyan). Although the Wesleyan Arminians doctrine has some close elements with the doctrine written in this book, it is still inadequate for a Missional Church. The focus of a Missional Church, as described in *Missional Reformation* (Olowe 2009), is societal cultural transformation; as such, a Missional Church engages the society. Calvinism, on the other hand, is unsuitable for a Missional Church. Executing the Great Commission is God's move for this generation. There are several problems with Calvinism, not only for a Missional Church, but for the Christian Body in general. Since its development in the 17th century, Calvinism has attracted a lot of controversies, making even philosophers and atheists to become "churchy", developing their own concepts. Let us look at some of the problems with Calvinism.

ETERNAL SECURITY

Calvinism teaches "once saved, always saved" (written as OSAS); that is, a person cannot lose his salvation. It uses the term "perseverance of the saints". The word "perseverance" means to "be steady" or theologically, to "continue in a state of grace to the end, leading to eternal salvation". The believer is assured that he is "secure" in Christ and will go to Heaven. The Westminster Confession of Faith (Chap. XVII, sec. 1) has defined perseverance of the saints as follows:

> They whom God hath accepted in His Beloved, effectually called and sanctified by his Spirit, can neither totally nor finally fall away from the state of grace; but shall certainly persevere therein to the end, and be eternally saved.

This view implies that man cannot fall from grace despite apostasy or unrepentant and habitual sin; the individual is truly saved if he accepted Christ at any point in the past. Jesus never promised anyone a free ride to Heaven without doing the Will of God.

Quoting Romans 12:1-3, Calvin claims that those chosen to receive grace will live good Christian lives. If an "elect" falls, Calvinism says that the person was not truly saved in the first place. This is like checking the answer and then working backward to solve a mathematical problem. But, ironically, all Calvinists will live as though they have been chosen, even if they have not been. It is still a false sense of security. In trying to dismiss any human efforts in securing a place in Heaven, Calvinists are turning a man to be a lazy robot or a puppet. Jesus' statements in Matthew 24:13 suggest that human efforts are needed. Calvinists' logic is too simplistic and not helpful to a believer in knowing what to do to live a good Christian life. In reference to Figure 9.1, Calvinists are saying that all chosen will successfully pass through the Salvation Life stage to the Kingdom Gate. They have defined a "chosen" as a believer who is able to reach the Kingdom Gate. The case of Judas Iscariot is a pain in the neck for Calvinists. Jesus said he was chosen.

> Jesus answered them, Have not I chosen you twelve, and one of you is a devil? John 6: 70

Daniel Corner writes:

> Regarding examples that contradict eternal security, perhaps the Apostle Judas Iscariot is most difficult for them. It seems that the facts revolving around this apostle must be distorted, twisted, read into and/or overlooked to maintain their erroneous view of the believer's security. Even illogical statements and Scripturally unsubstantiated statements surface to reconcile events in his life to eternal security!

There are several verses in the scripture that indicate that a believer can fall. Jesus said in Matthew 24:13 that only those who endure to the end will be finally saved; that is, enter into the Kingdom of God. This definitely indicates that human effort is required, in addition to God's grace and the intercession of Jesus, to reach the Kingdom Gate; although human effort is not needed to enter through the Salvation Gate. It is important to understand the difference. Once a believer receives Salvation, the journey to gain access to the Kingdom starts from there. The believer should be happy that he enters through the right Salvation Gate that leads to the Kingdom Gate; there are several other gates out there that do not lead to the Kingdom Gate.

LIMITED ATONEMENT

Calvinism teaches limited atonement (rather limited propitiation), which means Christ died for only a handful of mankind, called "the elect". Even Calvinists are divided on this doctrine; some remove the doctrine from the 5-Point Calvinism, leading to 4-Point Calvinism. The 5-Point Calvinists use the following verses in favor of Limited Atonement:

> And she shall bring forth a son, and thou shalt call his name JESUS: for he shall save his people from their sins. Matt 1: 21

> As the Father knoweth me, even so know I the Father: and I lay down my life for the sheep. John 10:15

> Greater love hath no man than this, that a man lay down his life for his friends. John 15:13

> Take heed therefore unto yourselves, and to all the flock, over the which the Holy Ghost hath made you overseers, to feed the church of God, which he hath purchased with his own blood. Acts 20:28

> Husbands, love your wives, even as Christ also loved the church, and gave himself for it; Eph 5:25

> So Christ was once offered to bear the sins of many; and unto them that look for him shall he appear the second time without sin unto salvation. Heb 9:28

These verses say that Christ died for a specific group of people - "the church," "His people," "His sheep," His friends." I believe the statements of Jesus have been taken out of context. Jesus is saying that even though He came to die for the sin of mankind, not all will believe; so, automatically His death covers only those who believe. Here are other reasons why propitiation is unlimited:

1. Jesus' death was primarily to remove the guilt of Adam's sin transmitted to his descendants.

> For as in Adam all die, so also in Christ all shall be made alive. 1 Cor. 15:22

Every man descends from Adam, so automatically Jesus' death is for all mankind.

2. In John 1:29, when John the Baptist saw Jesus coming towards him, he said: "*Behold the Lamb of God, which taketh away the sin of the world.*" John had no knowledge of specific "friends" of Jesus before he made the statement.

3. Jesus said in Luke 19:10:

> For the Son of man is come to seek and to save that which was lost. Luke 19: 10

The "elect" is not supposed to be lost. So the statement refers to all unbelievers in the world.
4. There are just too numerous biblical verses, some of which have been cited in Chapter 7 of this book, to prove *unlimited propitiation.*

DOCTRINE OF ELECTION

The Calvinists' doctrine of election, reprobation, and predestination are all in one package. The doctrines stem from Calvin's writings. In John Calvin's Institutes of Christian Religion, he wrote:

> Those, therefore, whom God passes by he reprobates, and that for no other cause but because he is pleased to exclude them from the inheritance which he predestines to his children...
>
> Now since the arrangement of all things is in the hand of God...He arranges... that individuals are born, who are doomed from the womb to certain death, and are to glorify him by their destruction...
>
> It was his good pleasure to doom to destruction...

UNCONDITIONAL ELECTION

Canons of Dordt define election as follows:

> Now election is the immutable purpose of God, whereby, before the foundations of the world were laid, he has, according to the most free good pleasure of his own will, of mere grace, chosen out of the whole human race, fallen by its own fault from its primeval integrity into sin and destruction, a certain number of persons, neither better nor more deserving than others but with them involved in a common misery, unto salvation in Christ; whom even from eternity he had appointed Mediator and Head of all the elect and the foundation of salvation; and therefore he has decreed to give them unto him to be saved.

This view, known as Calvinists doctrine of *Unconditional Election*, believes that God's election of people to salvation is done "with no conditions attached, either foreseen or otherwise." God elects people to salvation by His own sovereign choice and not because of some future action they will perform or condition they will meet.

As covered in Chapter 7; there are two elections. Calvinists are correct here that *initial election* is *unconditional.* However, *validated elections* are *conditional*, based on coming to Jesus and believing on Him. An initial election is merely a potential until validated.

REPROBATION

Calvinists doctrine of *Reprobation* is the most controversial and hated doctrine among Christians because it has no solid footing. It is a corollary of the doctrine of unconditional election. The Canons of Dordt distinguish election and reprobation because the Scripture "declares that not all men are elect but that certain ones have not been elected, or have been passed by in the eternal election of God". Calvin defended reprobation as follows:

> There could be no election without its opposite reprobation.... Those, therefore, God passes by he reprobates. Calvin (3.23.1)

Arthur Pink similarly defended the doctrine of reprobation:

> There cannot be an election without a rejection, a taking without a passing by, a choice without a refusal. As Psalm 78 expresses it, "He *refused* the tabernacle of Joseph, and *chose* not the tribe of Ephraim; but chose the tribe of Judah" (vv. 67, 68). Thus predestination includes both reprobation (the preterition or passing by of the non-elect, and then the foreordaining of them to condemnation—Jude 4—because of their sins) and election unto eternal life. (Arthur Pink – Doctrine of Election)

By their choice of words, does "passing by" necessarily interpret to "rejection"? Besides this, there is one major flaw in Calvinists doctrines of election and reprobation. Calvinists say election is unconditional and then say there cannot be an election without a rejection. In corollary, the rejection must also be unconditional. The point is, God is just; if there is to be a dual rejection and election, there must be a condition. It is true that there are rejections in the scripture, but there is always a reason – sin (evil works) of which everyone will be judged (Chapter 9). The passages below show the example of rejected angels because of rebellion against God.

> And the angels which kept not their first estate, but left their own habitation, he hath reserved in everlasting chains under darkness unto the judgment of the great day. Jude 1:6

> For if God spared not the angels that sinned, but cast them down to hell, and delivered them into chains of darkness, to be reserved unto judgment... 2 Pet 2:4

However, there are other variants of the doctrine. Evangelical Charles Finney posits a softer variant of the doctrine; he injects condition into reprobation which must also translate to conditional election.

> But what are the reasons why reprobates are rejected and lost? Because they are unwilling to be saved; that is, they are unwilling to be saved on the terms upon which alone God can consistently save them... It is their own act that leads him to send them to hell, and not his act in reprobating them. He reprobates and punishes them for their sins, because that, in spite of all he could wisely do to reclaim them, they would remain in their sins. (Finney – sermon on Reprobation)

Finney says a reprobate can still be saved.

> The salvation or damnation of the reprobate is suspended on their own choice.

The word "reprobate" is used in the New Testament by Paul only in Rom 1:28, 2 Cor 13:5-7, 2 Tim 3:8, and Tit 1:16. He never in any of those verses implied that God reprobates anyone from the foundation of the world. Calvin wrote:

> But if all whom the Lord predestines to death are naturally liable to sentence to death, of what injustice, pray, do they complain? Should all the sons of Adam come to dispute and contend with the Creator, because by his eternal providence they were before their birth doomed to perpetual destruction, when God comes to reckon with them, what will they be able to mutter against this defense? Calvin (3.23.3)

Calvin missed the point of Ezekiel 18:23,32. The possibility of *second election* (Chapter 7) provides the opportunity for those who were "passed by" to repent and receive salvation. God wants everyone saved. Jesus said:

> Likewise, I say unto you, there is joy in the presence of the angels of God over one sinner that repenteth.
> Luke 15: 10

DOCTRINE OF PREDESTINATION

Calvinists doctrine of predestination is derived from a combined doctrine of election and reprobation. Calvin defines predestination as,

> God's eternal decree, by which He compacted with himself what he willed to become of each man. For all are not created in equal condition; rather, eternal life is fore-

> ordained for some, eternal damnation for others (Inst. III, 21, 5).

The Westminster Confession of Faith (1643) says:

> By the decree of God, for the manifestation of his glory, some men and angels are predestinated unto everlasting life, and others foreordained to everlasting death.

In Reformed theology, the term "*double predestination*" has been used to refer to this dual concept of election and reprobation. It is also called Hyper Calvinism; God predestinates some to Heaven and predestinates others to hell. I could not find anywhere in the scripture where this "decree" or such statement is made; it is made from man's wisdom. This insults the sovereignty of God, the theology of which Calvinism seems to champion. There are too many questions the doctrine cannot answer. The more the Calvinists try to rationalize, the more they dig holes for themselves. The references cited to support the doctrine are:

> ROM 9:22 What if God, willing to shew his wrath, and to make his power known, endured with much longsuffering the vessels of wrath fitted to destruction: 23 And that he might make known the riches of his glory on the vessels of mercy, which he had afore prepared unto glory.

> EPH 1:5 Having predestinated us unto the adoption of children by Jesus Christ to himself, according to the good pleasure of his will, 6 To the praise of the glory of his grace, wherein he hath made us accepted in the beloved.

> PRO 16:4 The Lord hath made all things for himself: yea, even the wicked for the day of evil.

Evidently, it stems from the interpretation of Paul's writings. The Calvinists forget to cite Jesus, the author of Christianity:

> Not every one that saith unto me, Lord, Lord, shall enter into the Kingdom of Heaven; but he that doeth the will of my Father which is in Heaven. Matt. 7: 21

So, those who think they are "predestinated to Heaven" may not even have the boarding pass, if they don't do the will of God, which is the requirement into the Kingdom of God. We have stressed this point in this book and in "*Missional Reformation*" (Olowe 2009). If you are a lazy Christian without good works (doing one evil after another), hiding under this doctrine of predestination, thinking you are going to Heaven, you are having a false sense of security. There are several other quotations that contradict the interpretation of Paul's writings by the Calvinists. However, we need to quickly dispose off the verse in Proverbs that is added to justify their claim. "God made all things for Himself"; yes, God is the Creator of the person, but that does not mean He predestines him to be evil. If a man ignores the universal grace and chooses evil, God will still use him to accomplish His purpose. This explains the case of Pharaoh's hardened heart against the Israelites. God is not evil.

Paul's writing is interpreted out of context. Paul did not write that God predestinates any man to damnation. Some of his other writings indicate that he understands that man is condemned to damnation by his own choice and salvation is available to all men (see Rom. 1:16 for example). That is also central in the teaching of Jesus. Peter gives a good advice (2 Pet. 3:15-18) not to be led in error of interpretation; he says sometimes Paul's writings are difficult to crack. Here is the Application Bible's comment on the verses:

> The false teachers intentionally misused Paul's writings by twisting them to condone lawlessness. No doubt this made the teachers popular, because people always like to have their favorite sins justified, but the net effect was to totally destroy Paul's message... Peter warns his readers to avoid those wicked teachers by growing in the knowledge of Jesus. The better we know Jesus, the less attractive false teachings will be.

Another analysis by Cooper Abrams:

> Calvinism is contrary to God's grace itself, which stems from God's love and unmerited favor toward man. To accept Calvinism is to proclaim that God does not love all His creation and that nullifies His grace. It makes God unloving and unjust to most men on earth. It makes a man a robot in the matter of salvation. Calvinism restricts God's love to only a part of His creation and makes a lie out of God's statements that He loves the world (John 3:16). God is love and that is His very nature, therefore He cannot go against who He is and deny His love to some because He chooses not to love them. God says He is love. How then can the Calvinist say He is not? Not one word in the Bible limits God's love. God's love is offered freely, and is only limited by sinful men who will not accept His love. But that is not God's fault, but man's. John 3:15-16 states plainly "God so loved the world, that

he gave His only begotten Son." If you truly believe that statement from God's word, you cannot be a Calvinist. Man goes to hell because he is a sinner who rejects God, not because God decreed him to burn in hell and refuses to allow him to repent (Rom 1:18-23). It is a perversion of God's sovereignty and His grace to conclude He would violate His own nature and withhold His love toward the world. The question is simply this: "Does God love the world and did Jesus Christ, God incarnate in the flesh, come to the earth, suffer, and die for the sins of mankind?" The biblical answer is overwhelmingly YES! Then how can the Calvinist teach He didn't. On what basis does he teach that God did not extend His love to all men?

WHY CALVINISM IS UNSUITABLE FOR MISSIONAL CHURCH

Issues of election and predestination assume that God elects some people for salvation and the same God condemns others to damnation. All these happen before anyone is born. This doctrine can not be adopted by a Missional Church. A Missional Church engages the Society towards cultural transformation, thereby interacting with unbelievers with a goal of bringing them to Christ. Here are some of the limitations.

1. The doctrine is presumptuous about God and makes decisions for Him; Calvinism stands in the position of God and writes “decrees” that are not in the Bible.

2. Doctrine of predestination has no solid scriptural foundation; God usually reveals such important action to his prophets and others; no single prophet in the OT knew about it.

3. The doctrine of double predestination makes the entire life meaningless and God a joker.

4. According to Calvinism the good news of the Gospel is not good news for everyone.

5. The doctrine of double predestination limits God's supremacy and sovereignty (professed by Calvinists). It is like God is in partnership with satan, with both deciding whose soul to have.

6. If some men have been predestinated to salvation what is the necessity of the Great Commission? Why is it necessary to evangelize to someone that is already predestinated to hell? Some Calvinists actually say that evangelism is a mere show of faith; it is not intended to change anyone. Calvinism violates values of a Missional Church.

7. The doctrine encourages laziness and sin; why does anyone need to do good works?

8. What is the necessity to worship God?

9. In Calvinism, men must be predestined and effectually called unto faith by God before they will even wish to believe or wish to be justified; the concept of salvation itself makes it impossible to be born-again before first birth.

10. The doctrine gives room for a man to continue in doing evil once he declares for Christ;

11. Calvinism restricts God's love to only a part of His creation and makes a lie out of God's statements that He loves the world (Cooper Abrams).

12. Calvinism promises eternal security for the "elect"; it is a false sense of security.

13. The doctrine is presumptuous of the Holy Spirit; Calvinists believe that if you don't believe in predestination it is because the Holy Spirit has chosen not to reveal the truth of predestination to you. The Holy Spirit reveals the truth of predestination to "real believers"; so you must not be a real believer if you believe in free will (David Bennett).

14. The concept of justification is moot. Who is being judged?

15. The concept of sanctification is moot. Who needs it?

16. Special grace cannot be available to men if it is innate.

17. What is the essence of Jesus' death for mankind if God has predestinated who is going to hell?

18. Why are we talking about grace? What is it needed for?

19. What is the necessity of the commandments of God? Why does He say we must obey His commandments? If someone is predestinated to hell and he has no second chance of salvation, of what business has he with the commandments?

20. Why make confessional statements to accept Jesus as saviour? There is no need for that, since it is already predetermined that you are saved.

21. Double predestination implies that there are two sides of God: good and evil.

22-25. David Bennet (freewill-predestination.com) writes:

> 22. If God predestined everybody then why would He be emotional, angry if people and nations did exactly what they were designed by Him to do? (Bennet)
>
> 23. It may be demotivating for us to reach the lost if we believe everything is predetermined. If a person's salvation is already determined there is no real point in being proactive in the faith or urgency in preaching the Gospel. If your neighbor is unsaved Reformed Theology tells you that they will come to know Jesus or spend eternity in hell whether you tell them about God's plan for salvation or not; (Bennet).
>
> 24. According to Reformed Theology when someone, lets call her Molly, accepted Christ it wasn't really because of her own free will, but because God created her specifically to accept Christ, without a choice. Now suppose Molly's grown son dies without accepting Christ. Reformed Theology tells us that God created Molly's son specifically to spend eternity separated from God, in hell. Therefore all the years of prayer, anguish and hope that Molly's son would someday accept Christ was a waste of time. Her son was doomed in the womb and was created to be eternal kindling wood, a never-ending Duralog. It's one thing to have a loved one that rejects God because of his own choice, but it is another to believe that person

never had a chance because God never permitted or allowed them a chance. (Bennett)

25. To follow predestination to its logical conclusion we should not feel any sense of grief or sadness when an unsaved friend or relative dies and spends eternity in hell. Rather we should rejoice because the person is going to hell, just as God intended [for His pleasure] (Bennett).

26. Professor Hanko, a Reformed Theologian, writes:

To maintain double predestination is to close the door to any form of common [universal] grace, particularly to the idea that God's love, kindness and benevolence are shown to all men. But it works the other way around as well. If one is committed to common [universal] grace, in whatever form it takes, sovereign and double predestination falls by the wayside (Hanko 2009).

27. The doctrine of eternal security provides a false sense of security to young and innocent believers.

"Once saved, always saved" is a popular mantra of easy-believism that turns God's grace into lasciviousness by promising eternal life to those with ungodly lives. It has no Biblical basis as it is commonly used (letgodbetrue.com).

CONCLUDING REMARKS

For over 400 years now, the Church philosophers have been wrestling on few passages written by Paul that can be interpreted in several ways,

> Ye therefore, beloved, seeing ye know these things before, beware lest ye also, being led away with the error of the wicked, fall from your own steadfastness. But grow in grace, and in the knowledge of our Lord and Saviour Jesus Christ. To him be glory both now and for ever. Amen.2 Peter 3: 17-18

So, why task the brain so much to arrive at an irrational doctrine? Calvinism supports elitism and some Christians enjoy it and try to maintain it. The doctrine makes the essence of evangelizing questionable. What then is the essence of the Great Commission if some have been predestinated to hell? What for? Jesus did no say "Go find the elect". This doctrine can not work for a Full Gospel or Missional Church.

God is not the author of evil and so can not select some people and leave others to the ruins. "My thought towards you is to have everlasting end" (Jer 29:11). God loves everyone and wants everyone to be saved. What Paul is most likely saying in those passages is that those who are predestinated for specific commissions (such as revivalists or reformers) are automatically elected. God gives every man gifts of talent to succeed and not to fail. We have the Will to make the choice to succeed or not. Not everyone that is saved is predestined to carryout a special assignment or to be a preacher. A man has the Will to work against his destiny if he refuses to respond to the universal grace; this universal grace also assists man's Will to obtain the special grace. Some people are destined to work as full time ministers of God; some one not "predestinated" to work in the ministry can still receive salvation through the *second election*. God thinks of good for everyone; it is our choice that lands us wherever we find ourselves when we don't respond to the universal grace and urging of the Holy Spirit.

Let us interpret the Bible with simplicity and rationality and not be too academic with it, and importantly, asking for guidance from the Holy Spirit. In the New Testament, Paul is the only one that uses the term "predestination" in 4 passages (Rom 8:29-30, Eph 1:5,11), and he is the only one that uses the term "reprobate" in 6 passages (Rom 1:28, 2Cor 13:5-7, 2Tim 3:8, Tit 1:16). In the Old Testament, there is only one occurrence of the term "reprobate" (Jer 6:30), and the term "predestination" is not used at all. Calvinists doctrine of double predestination is using man's wisdom to (mis)interpret few passages that Paul wrote and whereas there are several passages (even many by Paul himself) that imply otherwise.

Calvinists' doctrine of Sovereignty and of total depravity of man certainly need some re-work, but the reprobation and double predestination doctrines should be thrown out of the Church.

> Yet if thou warn the wicked, and he turn not from his wickedness, nor from his wicked way, he shall die in his iniquity; but thou hast delivered thy soul. Ezekiel 3:19

CONCLUSION

THE Holy Spirit directed me to study the entire book of Job during my research. I believe this book is important in our understanding God. I have provided my analysis as far as my knowledge and wisdom can take me. I encourage others to study this book of Job with the guidance of the Holy Spirit (not in flesh), may be God will make further revelations about Himself and His creations. I believe there are a lot to learn from the book. Man can never totally figure God out.

God has always spoken through people and will continue to do so. Just as the Lord used the Apostles in the first century to provide the base doctrine of Christianity, He has used others over the centuries to improve on it, and He will continue to use men towards a sound doctrine. God has never revealed all His plans to a single person on earth. We should not get stagnant with the doctrines of the first century Apostles; the Lord never meant it to be that way. As the world advances technologically, so also we must advance spiritually as God releases His plans to individuals. It is good that we have women ministers now and we have not gotten stalled with the doctrine that women are to remain as pew members.

This written project, which includes the *Missional Reformation* book and this *Grace Theology* book, has been executed within a year of intense revelations. In this particular book, we see so many things go in pairs:

	Chap	**Pair**
Great Commandments	8	First and Second
Gospel of God	8	Salvation and Good works
Will of God	5,8	Salvation and Good works
Grace of God	3,6	Universal and Special
Election	7	First and Second
Types of Works	8	Physical and Spiritual
Sins to be justified of	9	Primary and Secondary
Gates to Eternal Kingdom	9	Initial and Final salvation gates
Obstacles to the Kingdom gate	9	Spiritual battles and Sins
Overcoming secondary sins	9	Repentance and Good works

In no way can I conclude that the doctrine presented here is perfect, but I am sure it lays a good foundation and can be perfected. I welcome suggestions and discussions, especially from theologians. God be with the Church.

BIBLIOGRAPHY

Abrams, Cooper P.; *Is Calvinism or Arminianism Biblical? A Biblical Explanation of the Doctrine of Election*, http://bible-truth.org/election.htm

Adelaja, Sunday; *Church Shift*, Charisma house, 2008

Ahab, Calvin; *Grace Versus Works and Predestination*, Mar 04 2003, http://everything2.com/

Application Study Bible (KJV), Tyndale House Publishers inc., 2004

Augustin, Aurelius; *A Treatise On The Predestination of the Saints*, Hippo, 490 AD

Bacote, Vincent and Pylman, Daniel, *A Neo-Kuyperian Assist to the Emergent Church*, Wheaton College, 2008, www.vanguardchurch.com

Bainton, Roland; *The Age of the Reformation*, Princeton, NJ: D. Van Nostrand Company, Inc., 1956

Baker, Robert A.; *A Summary of Christian History*. Revised by John M. Landers. Nashville: Broadman and Holman Publishers, 1994

Barna, George; *The second coming of the Church: A blue print for survival*, Word Publishing Nashville, 1998

Barrett, David; *World Christian Encyclopedia*, 2001

Barrett, David and Johnson, Todd M.; *International Bulletin of Missionary Research*, January 2009

Bavinck, Herman; *Our Reasonable Faith*, Wm. B. Eerdmans Publishing Co. (Grand Rapids), 1956

Bennett, David; *Predestined for Free Will*, 2004, www.freewill-predestination.com/freewill.html

Bernbaum, John A. and Steer, Simon M.; *Why Work? Careers and Employment in Biblical Perspective*, Baker, Grand Rapids, 1986

Boettner, Loraine, *The Reformed Doctrine of Predestination*, (not accessed but an important reference; he is the author of Calvinist doctrine of predestination)

Brown, Peter; *Augustine of Hippo: A Biography*. Berkeley and Los Angeles: Univ. of California Press, 1969

Calvin, John; *Institutes of the Christian Religion*, Westminster Press: Philadelphia, 1960.

Cope, Landa; *An Introduction to The Old Testament Template*, http://readingsandreflections.blogspot.com/2007/12/introduction-to-old-testament-template.html

Cope, Landa; *The Old Testament Template*, Template Institute, 2007

Corner, Dan; *The Believer's Conditional Security*, Evangelical Outreach, 2000

Corner, Dan; *The Apostle Judas Iscariot*, www.evangelicaloutreach.org/judas.htm

Corner, Dan; *John 6:37-39 - Another Eternal Security Misuse of Scripture*, www.evangelicaloutreach.org/john637.htm

Craig, Kenneth W.; *The Plan of Redemption*, 2007, www.windmillministries.org

Cunningham, Loren; *Winning God's Way*, YWAM Publishing, 1988

Cunningham, William; *Historical Theology*. Edinburgh: The Banner of Truth Trust, 1979. Two volumes. Reprint of 1862 edition.

DeVries, Paul; *The Gift of Time*, June 14, 2009, www.backtogodradio.com/messages.php?action=Story&message_id=485

Finney, Charles; *Trusting in God's Mercy*, Sermon, May 7, 1845

Finney, Charles; *Reprobation*, Sermon, www.Gospeltruth.net/1836SOIS/11sois_reprobation.htm

Hanko, Herman; Hoeksema, Homer, and Van Baren, Gise J.; *The Five Points of Calvinism*, Reformed Free Publishing Association, 1976

Hanko, Herman C.; *Another Look at Common Grace: Restraint of Sin and General Revelation*, www.prca.org/prtj/apr96c.html

Hanko, Herman C.; *Common vs. Particular Grace*, April 3, 2009, common-grace-considered.blogspot.com

Hanko, Herman C.; *The "Free Offer" of the Gospel*, April 6, 2009, common-grace-considered.blogspot.com

Hanko, Herman C.; *Election and Reprobation Denied*, August 31, 2009, common-grace-considered.blogspot.com

Hanko, Herman C.; *Is General Revelation a matter of Common Grace?* October 14, 2009, common-grace-considered.blogspot.com

Haugh, Jay; *Role of Sacrifice Within the Old Testament*, Sept. 18, 2006, satisfiedingod.blogspot.com

Hodges, Zane C.; *The Gospel Under Siege*, Redencin Viva, 1992, zhodges.cust.he.net/paul/paul.html

Hopfl, Harro. *The Christian Polity of John Calvin.* Cambridge University Press: Cambridge, 1982

Horton, Michael; *Christless Christianity: The Alternative Gospel of the American Church*, Baker Book House, 2008

Isaac, Donald J.; *Work and Christian Calling*, www.directionjournal.org/article/?1308

Just, Felix; *Paul and James on Faith and Works*, www.catholic-resources.org/Bible/Paul-James.htm

Kirby, Peter; *Ignatius of Antioch*, Early Christian Writings, 2 Feb. 2006; http://www.earlychristianwritings.com/ignatius.html

Kirby, Peter; *Polycarp*, Early Christian Writings, 2 Feb. 2006; http://www.earlychristianwritings.com/martyrdompolycarp.html

Kuyper, Abraham; *Lectures on Calvinism*: The Stone Lectures of 1898, Six Lectures Delivered at Princeton University, 1898 under the auspices of the L. P. Stone Foundation

Kuyper, Abraham; The *Work of the Holy Spirit*, (1888; American edition 1900) vol. 3

Long, Jimmy; *Generating Hope: A strategy for reaching the post-modern generation, in Telling The Truth*, Zondervan Publishing House, 2000

Masselink, William; *General Revelation and Common Grace*, W. B. Eerdmans Pub. Co. (Grand Rapids), 1953

Matthews, Mary W.; *The Difference Between Soul and Spirit*, www.extremelysmart.com/insight/theology/soul&spirit.php

McNeill, John T.; *The History and Character of Calvinism.* Oxford University Press, London, 1954.

Munroe, Myles, *Pursuit of purpose*, www.youtube.com/

Murdock, Mike, *365 Wisdom Keys*, www.thoughts.com/bubbles22/blog/365-wisdom-keys-of-mike-murdock-137103

Murray, John; *The sovereignty of God*, www.the-highway.com/sovereignty_Murray1.html

Olowe, Abi, *Great Revivals, Great Revivalist – Joseph Ayo Babalola*, Omega Publishers, 2007

Olowe, Abi, *Missional Reformation for Discipling Nations*, Omega Publishers, 2009

Paine, Thomas, *Remarks on Romans IX. 18-21*,

Parsley, Rod; *Culturally Incorrect*, 2007, ISBN: 978-1-5995-1013-2

Perman, Matt; *If God is sovereign, Why Do Anything?*, www.mountainretreatorg.net/articles/sov.html

Pink, Arthur; *The Sovereignty of God*, Providence Baptist Ministries, 1949, www.pbministries.org/books/pink

Pink, Arthur; *The Attributes of God*, Providence Baptist Ministries, 1949, www.pbministries.org/books/pink

Pink, Arthur; *The Total Depravity of man*, Providence Baptist Ministries, 1949, www.pbministries.org/books/pink

Pink, Arthur; *The Doctrine of Election*, Providence Baptist Ministries, 1949, www.pbministries.org/books/pink

Placher, William; *A History of Christian Theology*, Westminster Press: Philadelphia, 1983.

Redekop, Calvin and Bender, Urie A., *Who Am I? What Am I? Searching for Meaning in Your Work,* Academie, Grand Rapids, 1988

Reno, R.R.; *Brain Science and the Soul*, FIRST THINGS, October 20, 2008, www.firstthings.com/onthesquare/?p=1201

Rhodes, Ron; *The Extent of the Atonement: Limited Atonement Versus Unlimited Atonement,* Reasoning from the Scriptures Ministries, http://home.earthlink.net/~ronrhodes/Atonement.html

Ritchie, Mark S.; *The story of the Church, notes from the Church History classes taught in 1997-1999 at Community Bible Chapel*, 2005, Richardson, Texas, http://www.ritchies.net/churchhi.htm

Ross, Allen; *Holiness to the Lord: A Guide to the Exposition of the Book of Leviticus*, Grand Rapids: Baker Academics, 2002

Schaff, Philip; *History of the Christian Church.* 8 volumes, Grand Rapids: William B. Eerdmans Publishing Company, 1979

Stewart, David J.; *Good Works Verses Grace*, www.jesus-is-savior.com/salvation_webpages/18-good_works_verses_grace.htm

Stewart, Tom; *What Is Mercy?*, December 28, 1999, www.whatsaiththescripture.com

Terpstra Charles J., *Abraham Kuyper, Developer and Promoter of Common Grace*, The Mountain Retreat, Vol. 75; No. 2; October 15, 1998, www.mountainretreatorg.net/articles/kuyper_terp.html

Thompson, Bert; *The Mercy and Grace of God*, Apologetics Press, January 1997, www.apologeticspress.org/articles/186

Tucker, Dennis; *The Importance of Work*, www.truthfactor.com

Vine, W.E.; *An Expository Dictionary of New Testament Words*, Old Tappan, NJ: Revell, 1940

Ward, Barbara; *The Rich Nations and the Poor Nations,* Norton, New York, 1962

Warren, Rick; *The Purpose Driven Life*, Zondervan, 2002

Webber, Robert E., *Younger Evangelicals, Facing the Challenges of the New World*

Wesley, John, *Justification by Faith*, sermon (text from the 1872 edition - Thomas Jackson, editor), new.gbgm-umc.org

Wesley, John, *On Perfection*, sermon (text from the 1872 edition - Thomas Jackson, editor), new.gbgm-umc.org

Wesley, John, *On Predestination*, sermon (text from the 1872 edition - Thomas Jackson, editor), new.gbgm-umc.org

Wesley, John, *On the Fall of Man*, sermon (text from the 1872 edition - Thomas Jackson, editor), new.gbgm-umc.org

Wesley, John, *satan's Devices*, sermon (text from the 1872 edition - Thomas Jackson, editor), new.gbgm-umc.org

Wesley, John, *The Good Steward*, sermon (text from the 1872 edition - Thomas Jackson, editor), new.gbgm-umc.org

Willard, Samuel; *The Decrees of God*, Sermon 15 July, 1690, www.puritansermons.com/willard/willard1.htm

Zeolla, Gary F., *Soul, Spirit, and Knowing God*, www.fitnessforoneandall.com/dtl/dtl/treatise/soul-spirit-1.htm

INTERNET BY SUBJECT

Church History: Accusations against Christians, chi.Gospelcom.net/GLIMPSEF/Glimpses/glmps010.shtml

Church History: Gnosticism, chi.Gospelcom.net/lives_events/more/gnosticism.shtml

Church History: Navigation and exploration: AD 1415-1460, www.historyworld.net/wrldhis/PlainTextHistories.asp?ParagraphID=gpp

Church History: Timeline, www.saintignatiuschurch.org/timeline.html

Dominionism: Neo-Kuyperian Spheres, Discernment Research Group, 2007, herescope.blogspot.com/2007/06/neo-kuyperian-spheres.html

Dominionism: Seven Apostolic Spheres, Discernment Research Group, 2007, herescope.blogspot.com/2007/06/

Gospel of the Kingdom, www.gnmagazine.org/booklets/GK

God's Grace and Human Works, www.justforcatholics.org/a41.htm

Grace, Faith, and Good Works, www.acts17-11.com/grace_faith.html

Irenaeus Against Heresies Book IV, www.ccel.org

Justification by Faith and by Works, www.middletownbiblechurch.org/doctrine/JamesPau.htm

Old Testament Sacrifices and Offerings, www.americanbible.org/absport/news/item.php?id=58

Westminster Confession of Faith, www.freepres.org/WCF.htm, www.reformed.org/documents/wcf_with_proofs/

INDEX

Similar books by the author

If you enjoyed *Grace Theology*, you need to get these two books:

ISBN: 978-0-9795299-0-0 ISBN: 978-0-9795299-4-8

PUBLISHED BY

OMEGA PUBLISHERS

HOUSTON, TEXAS, U.S.A.

Useful Resources

These books: www.missionalreformation.com
www.greatrevivals.com

ChurchShift movement: www.churchshift.org
www.churchshiftusa.org

www.ingramcontent.com/pod-product-compliance
Lightning Source LLC
LaVergne TN
LVHW012330100826
845148LV00017B/1663

* 9 7 8 0 9 7 9 5 2 9 9 5 5 *